Nadja Brize, Amel Selmi

Grundwissen Englisch inklusiv

Wortschatz 5. Klasse Inklusionsmaterial

PERSEN

Die Autoren

Nadja Brize ist seit 2011 im Gemeinsamen Lernen aktiv. Sie unterrichtet Kinder mit und ohne sonderpädagogischen Unterstützungsbedarf an einer Gesamtschule in Bochum. Ihre Fächer sind Englisch, Kunst und Hauswirtschaft in der Sekundarstufe I. Zudem ist sie in der staatlichen Lehrerfortbildung zum Thema Inklusion tätig.

Amel Selmi ist seit Jahren im Gemeinsamen Lernen aktiv. An der Erich Kästner Gesamtschule in Bochum unterrichtet sie seit 2013 Kinder mit und ohne sonderpädagogischen Unterstützungsbedarf in den Fächern Englisch und Sport. Zudem ist sie eingebunden in die schulinterne Erstellung eines Leitfadens zur praxisorientierten Umsetzung inklusiven Unterrichts. Im Rahmen der konzeptionellen Ausrichtung erstellt sie Vorschläge, wie Inklusion effektiv und schülerorientiert umgesetzt werden kann.

Gedruckt auf umweltbewusst gefertigtem, chlorfrei gebleichtem und alterungsbeständigem Papier.

1. Auflage 2017

Covergrafik: Stefan Lucas
Satz: Satzpunkt Ursula Ewert GmbH, Bayreuth

ISBN: 978-3-403-23687-0

www.persen.de

Inhaltsverzeichnis

1. Vorwort 5

2. Methodisch-didaktische Hinweise 5
- 2.1 Sprache und Kommunikation 5
- 2.2 Kompetenzerwartungen 5
- 2.3 Inklusion und Lernen 6
- 2.4 Zu den Übungen 6
- 2.5 Merkmale auf einen Blick 7

1 Kopiervorlagen
my family

Übersichtsseite 8
family words 1 9
family words 2 10
family words 3 11
family words 1 12
family words 2 13
family words 3 14
family tree 1 15
family tree 2 16
family tree 17

2 rooms in a house

Übersichtsseite 18
rooms in a house 1 19
rooms in a house 2 20
rooms in a house 3 21
rooms in a house 4 22
rooms in a house 5 23
rooms in a house 1 24
rooms in a house 2 25
rooms in a house 3 26
rooms in a house 4 27
rooms in a house 5 28

3 my school

Übersichtsseite 29
subjects 1 30
subjects 2 31
subjects 32
school things 1 33
school things 2 34
school things 3 35
at school 1 36
at school 2 37
at school 3 38
at school 4 39
school things 1 40
school things 2 41
at school 1 42
at school 2 43
at school 3 44

4 my free time

Übersichtsseite 45
my free time 1 46
my free time 2 47
my free time 3 48
my free time 4 49
my free time 1 50
my free time 2 51
my free time 3 52
my free time 4 53
my free time 5 54

5 my pets and animals

Übersichtsseite 55
my pets and animals 1 56
my pets and animals 2 57
my pets and animals 3 58
my pets and animals 4 59
my pets and animals 1 60
my pets and animals 2 61
my pets and animals 3 62
my pets and animals 4 63
my pets and animals 5 64

6 days and months

Übersichtsseite 65
days and months 1 66
days and months 2 67
days and months 3 68
days and months 4 69
dates 70
days and months 1 71
days and months 2 72
days and months 3 73
dates 74

Inhaltsverzeichnis

7 times

Übersichtsseite 75
times 1 76
times 2 77
times 1 78
times 2 79

8 numbers and colours

Übersichtsseite 80
numbers 1 81
numbers 2 82
numbers 1 83
numbers 2 84
colours 1 85
colours 2 86
colours 1 87
colours 2 88

9 my party

Übersichtsseite 89
my party 1 90
my party 2 91
my party 3 92
my party 1 93
my party 2 94
my party 3 95

10 food

Übersichtsseite 96
food 1 97
food 2 98
food 3 99
food 4 100
food 5 101
food 6 102
food 1 103
food 2 104
food 3 105
food 4 106

11 shopping and clothes

Übersichtsseite 107
shopping and clothes 1 108
shopping and clothes 2 109
shopping and clothes 3 110
shopping and clothes 4 111
shopping and clothes 1 112
shopping and clothes 2 113
shopping and clothes 3 114
shopping and clothes 4 115

Abbildungsverzeichnis 116

Grau unterlegte Arbeitsblätter im Inhaltsverzeichnis sind die Arbeitsblätter für die Schüler mit sonderpädagogischem Förderbedarf.

Inhalt der CD:
- **alle Kopiervorlagen als editierbare Word-Dateien**
- **Lösungen im PDF-Format**

Vorwort / Methodisch-didaktische Hinweise

1. Vorwort

Das vorliegende Übungsbuch eignet sich für die 5. Jahrgangsstufe und ist für inklusiven Englischunterricht ausgelegt. Es beinhaltet alle vorgesehenen Themen und Anforderungen des Lehrplans für die Klasse 5 und deckt somit den gesamten hier zu erlernenden Wortschatzbereich ab. Themenbezogen angelehnt an das Lehrwerk, ermöglicht es den Schülern[1], mithilfe unterschiedlicher Übungen Vokabeln zu erlernen und den erlernten Wortschatz zu vertiefen. Die Materialien können jedoch auch lehrwerksunabhängig eingesetzt werden.

Eine individuelle Unterrichtsgestaltung steht hierbei im Mittelpunkt, sodass die Materialien in unterschiedlich strukturierten Klassen eingesetzt und individuell auf die jeweiligen Lerngruppen abgestimmt werden können. Insbesondere Inklusionsklassen mit heterogenen Lerngeschwindigkeiten und Förderniveaus profitieren vom Einsatz der hier vorliegenden Kopiervorlagen. Leistungsübergreifende Kooperation und gemeinsames Lernen werden auch innerhalb der Differenzierung gefördert. Eine übersichtliche Darstellung des Vokabulars ermöglicht den Schülern, die jeweilige Unterrichtsthematik der Fachbücher schnell zu erfassen und zu vertiefen. Lehrern werden Materialien an die Hand gegeben, um auf eine einfache Art strukturiert, binnendifferenziert und individualisiert jahrgangsspezifische Themen zu üben und zu vertiefen.

[1] Wir sprechen hier wegen der besseren Lesbarkeit von Schülern bzw. Lehrern in der verallgemeinernden Form. Selbstverständlich sind auch alle Schülerinnen und Lehrerinnen gemeint.

2. Methodisch-didaktische Hinweise

2.1 Sprache und Kommunikation

Für Fremdsprachen und somit auch für den Englischunterricht ist das Erlernen eines Wortschatzes unabdingbar, um elementare Kommunikationsstrategien auszuführen, Texte zu verstehen und überhaupt in Kommunikation treten zu können. Durch die in diesem Übungsband in thematischen Zusammenhängen geordneten Vokabeln erfahren Schüler früh, ihren Grundwortschatz zu erweitern und sich in alltagsbezogenen Themen zu verständigen und mitzuteilen. Diese Struktur und die Kombination mit bildlichen Darstellungen ermöglichen ein vereinfachtes Erlernen und spontanes Nachschlagen von Vokabeln, dessen Einsatz die Grundlage dafür bildet, eine Fremdsprache anwenden und somit in ihr kommunizieren zu können.

2.2 Kompetenzerwartungen

Dieser Band ist auf die Kompetenzerwartungen der 5. Jahrgangsstufe ausgerichtet. Kleinschrittig werden die vorgesehenen Themen, Inhalte und entsprechenden Arbeitsaufträge Kapitel für Kapitel abgedeckt.

Die Schüler können …

- über ihre Familie sprechen und diese vorstellen
- ihr Zimmer beschreiben und Gegenstände in selbigem benennen
- über ihre Schule sprechen und Gegenstände im Klassenraum und in der Schultasche benennen
- über ihre Hobbies und ihre Freizeitgestaltung berichten
- Tiere benennen
- die Uhrzeit (Monate / Wochentage) nennen, Zahlen / Ordnungszahlen aussprechen
- die eigene Geburtstagsparty planen
- über ihr Lieblingsessen sprechen
- über Kleidung sprechen

2.3 Inklusion und Lernen

Die in diesem Band vorliegenden Übungen und Texte sind unter besonderer Berücksichtigung der Bedürfnisse eines inklusiven Unterrichts erstellt worden. Diese Unterrichtsform stellt viele Lehrer vor besondere Herausforderungen, da alle Schüler möglichst individuell und leistungsdifferent gefördert werden sollen. Aus diesem Grund ist dieses Vokabel-Übungsbuch derart gestaltet worden, inklusiven Unterricht für Lehrer und auch für die Schüler leistungsheterogen und in seiner Struktur vereinheitlicht nachhaltig zu ermöglichen.

Unterschiedliche Aufgabentypen und Niveau-Differenzierungen stellen sicher, dass die Kopiervorlagen für den gesamten Klassenverband verwendet werden können. Die übersichtliche Strukturierung der Inhalte und Themen bietet den Lehrern einen schnellen Zugriff auf Materialien sowohl für lernstarke als auch für lernschwache Schüler. So eignet sich dieser Band hervorragend zum Einsatz in inklusiven Lerngruppen. Aber auch unabhängig davon können diese Materialien für Klassen unterschiedlicher Lernniveaus eingesetzt werden. Die sich unterscheidenden Übungen helfen, mehr Sicherheit in den verschiedenen Leistungsniveaus im Umgang mit dem englischen Wortschatz zu erlangen, das Vokabular zu erweitern und zu vertiefen. Hierbei motivieren klar strukturierte Lerneinheiten zum Arbeiten und bieten besonders für lernschwache Schüler einen vereinfachten Zugang, um Lerninhalte zu erfassen und die Übungen umzusetzen. Dies wurde derart umgesetzt, dass die Kopiervorlagen für Schüler mit Förderbedarf weniger abstrakt und durch Vereinfachungen oder Unterstützung angeleitet sind. Viele Illustrationen, Vorgaben, Beispielsätze und Einsatzübungen unterstützen den Prozess, den Unterrichtsstoff inklusiv und zeitgleich zu vermitteln. Kapitel für Kapitel wird das wichtige Vokabular wiederholt und vielfältige Übungen zur Vertiefung des Wortschatzes angeboten.

2.4 Zu den Übungen

Im vorliegenden Übungsbuch werden unterschiedliche Übungen und Texte angeboten: Einsatzübungen, Zuordnungsübungen, Bildbeschreibungen und kurze Texte mit Fragen zum Verständnis.

Die Übungen sind unabhängig vom Lehrwerk einsetzbar, decken jedoch die spezifischen und lehrwerkrelevanten Themen ab. Sie sind sowohl für lernstarke als auch für lernschwache Gruppen konzipiert. Es ist zudem jederzeit möglich, lernschwache Gruppen auch die schwierigeren Kopiervorlagen bearbeiten zu lassen, wenn der Lernstoff beherrscht wird und der Wortschatz vertieft werden soll. Kopiervorlagen für lernschwache Schüler sind zusätzlich mit zweisprachigen Aufgabenanleitungen versehen. Bitte beachten Sie, dass die Erläuterung der Aufgaben zum besseren Verständnis und zur besseren Lesbarkeit sinngemäß und nicht wortwörtlich übersetzt wurden. Das erleichtert den lernschwächeren Schülern die Arbeit erheblich und versetzt sie in die Lage, die Aufgaben selbstständig zu bearbeiten.

Für einen schnellen Überblick ist jedem Kapitel eine Übersichtsseite mit allen relevanten Vokabeln themenspezifisch vorangestellt. So können Vokabeln strukturiert gelernt und gezielt nachgeschlagen werden. Bildliche Unterstützungen bieten zusätzliche Hilfe für Schüler, vereinfachen den Arbeitsprozess und verhelfen so zu einer schnelleren Umsetzung der Aufgaben. Mit der beiliegenden CD bietet sich Lehrern die Gelegenheit, weitere Übungsmöglichkeiten zu erstellen: Alle Arbeitsblätter stehen als veränderbare Word-Datei zur Verfügung. So können z. B. Arbeitsblätter erstellt werden, die zusätzlich zum Üben oder auch für Vokabeltests eingesetzt werden können.

2.5 Merkmale auf einen Blick

- Abdeckung aller schulrelevanten Themen der 5. Jahrgangsstufe
- einfache und klare Strukturierung
- Ermöglicht selbständiges Arbeiten
- Übersichtsseite zu jedem Thema
- themenbezogenes Vokabular
- systematische Wiederholung und Festigung des Wortschatzes
- Übungsmaterial sowohl für regulären als auch für Unterricht in Inklusionsklassen (für Schüler mit Förderbedarf geeignet)
- kleinschrittige und vereinfachte Aufgaben
- leistungsdifferenziertes Arbeitsmaterial
- Zweisprachige Arbeitsaufträge für Schüler mit sonderpädagogischem Förderbedarf
- unterstützende Illustrationen

Bedeutung der Aufgabennummerierung

1 Aufgaben mit dieser Markierung sind für Regelschüler entwickelt worden, das heißt für Schüler, die nach den Anforderungen der allgemeinen Schule unterrichtet und bewertet werden. Sie orientieren sich an den allgemeingültigen Kompetenzen für den Englischunterricht.

2 Aufgaben mit dieser Markierung sind für Förderschüler entwickelt worden, das heißt für Schüler mit sonderpädagogischem Förderbedarf, die zieldifferent unterrichtet werden.

my family – Übersichtsseite

father (Vater)
husband (Ehemann)

mother (Mutter)
wife (Ehefrau)

parents (Eltern)

married to (verheiratet)

divorced (geschieden)

dead (gestorben)

son (Sohn)
nephew (Neffe)
grandson (Enkelsohn)
grandchild (Enkelkind)
single (Single)

daughter (Tochter)
cousin (Cousin / Cousine)
niece (Nichte)
granddaughter (Enkeltochter)

aunt (Tante)

uncle (Onkel)

stepfather (Stiefvater)

stepmother
(Stiefmutter)

grandmother (Großmutter)

grandfather (Großvater)

family words 1

1 Find the family words. You can use the ideas in the box.
Finde die Familien-Wörter. Du kannst die Ideen in der Box verwenden.

J	D	Y	Q	V	C	Q	S	C	S	J	C	E
G	R	A	N	D	D	A	U	G	H	T	E	R
R	Y	L	U	P	W	S	B	F	Y	P	F	W
H	N	R	V	U	H	U	S	B	A	N	D	T
U	D	A	E	D	K	T	W	P	K	J	P	S
D	E	A	D	H	S	I	N	G	L	E	M	C
D	V	X	W	C	R	X	M	N	B	Q	P	I
S	G	R	A	N	D	S	O	N	D	Y	D	D
M	W	G	E	D	A	D	N	V	U	E	F	C
J	G	W	F	D	A	U	G	H	T	E	R	G
M	S	I	T	R	Y	S	M	F	I	M	T	W
W	C	F	O	L	D	I	V	O	R	C	E	D
W	F	E	Q	Q	V	N	Q	G	I	Q	L	V

wife husband divorced dead
single daughter granddaughter
grandson

2 Find the family words. Look at the words in the box.
Finde die Familien-Wörter. Schau dir die Wörter in der Box an.

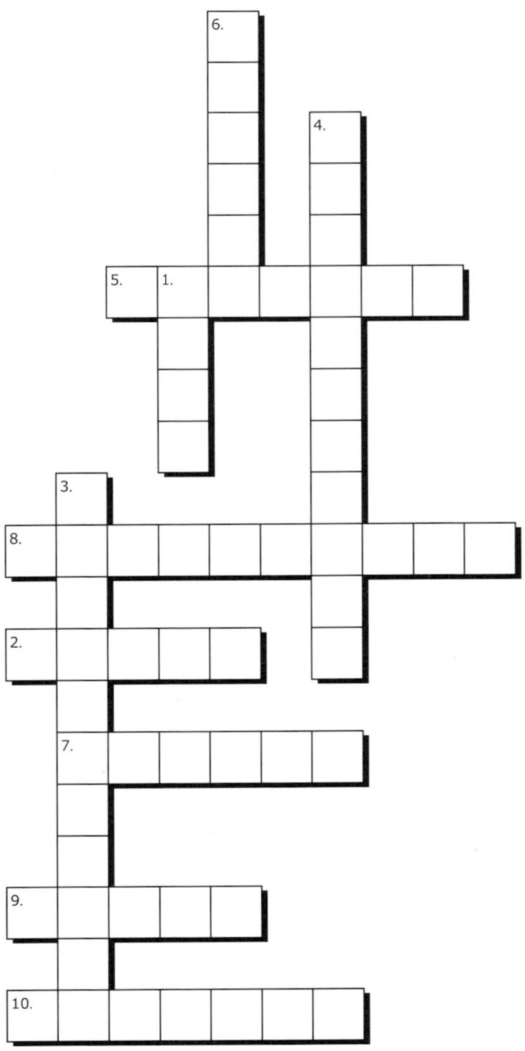

1. She is the sister of your mother.
2. He is the brother of your mother.
3. He is the dad of your dad.
4. She is the mother of your mother.
5. Your mother and your father are your ...
6. She is the daughter of your grandmother.
7. He is the son of your grandmother.
8. You are not the child, but the … of your granddad.
9. You are the … of your parents.
10. You can have a sister or a …

mother uncle aunt grandfather
parents child father grandchild
grandmother brother

family words 2

3 Find the word pairs and colour them.
Finde die Wortpaare und male sie in der gleichen Farbe an.

mother	aunt	sister	father	brother	uncle
grandma	married	niece	granddad	nephew	divorced

4 Read the text and answer the questions.
Lies den Text und beantworte die Fragen, indem du den richtigen Namen dahinter schreibst.

This is Liz's family.

Hi, I am Liz and this is my family: my parents, **Latisha and Michael**, and my **brother Dan**. My mother works in a hospital and my father works in a big supermarket. He is the manager. **My brother is 11 years old**. We have a **big house in London** and **we have a dog**. His name is Sharky. Our dog loves playing outside in the garden. My mum always tells me to keep my room tidy, especially when granddad and grandmother come to visit us. They live next to us in **London**. But they don't have a big house.

This is Lisa's family.

Hi, I am Lisa and I am **12 years old**. This my family. My mum and dad are divorced. I live with my mother in a small flat in **Bristol**, but I have my own room. My mother's name is Susan. My father's name is Daniel. I have no brother and no sister. We always have fun together. I have a **little cat**. Her name is **Pitty**. She **loves to sleep in my bed** and she always wakes me up. My mother works in the **book shop** of my uncle. My aunt has no time to help him, because she must take care of my little cousins. They are still babies.

family words 3

Who is it? Wer ist es?

1. She has got a brother and his name is Dan. *Liz*

2. She lives in Bristol. ______________________

3. What's the name of her father? ______________________

4. Her father's name is Michael. ______________________

5. Her brother is 11 years old. ______________________

6. She is 12 years old. ______________________

7. She has got a little cat and her name is Pitty. ______________________

8. Her mother works in the book shop. ______________________

5 Bring a picture or draw your family. Write about your family and write down the names.
Bring ein Bild deiner Familie mit oder male eins. Schreibe über deine Familie. Ergänze hierfür die Sätze.

This is my family.

1. My parents are ______________ and ______________.

2. My brother's name is ______________. My sister's name is ______________.

3. Our house / flat is in ______________.

4. My grandmother and grandfather live in ______________.

5. I have got a pet. His name is ______________.

family words 1

① **Find the family words.**

W	S	K	X	X	D	S	G	R	A	N	D	S	O	N	T
P	V	L	E	O	W	F	W	F	J	J	A	E	T	L	U
G	C	Q	H	B	T	M	F	S	I	N	G	L	E	S	O
S	R	D	H	J	S	A	I	M	V	A	T	Q	X	G	R
J	C	R	P	V	B	J	I	X	V	E	V	K	K	D	J
D	E	M	M	P	M	D	E	A	D	S	A	O	H	A	E
I	U	B	B	T	O	M	U	H	P	A	X	O	L	U	S
V	K	H	V	Y	I	Y	L	B	F	C	O	N	Y	G	R
O	L	Q	R	U	V	Q	O	T	Q	F	R	W	R	H	X
R	T	S	M	U	S	S	H	L	B	K	S	Q	W	T	K
C	N	B	G	R	A	N	D	D	A	U	G	H	T	E	R
E	S	L	X	R	C	T	I	N	D	T	H	Q	F	R	S
D	Q	R	D	H	U	S	B	A	N	D	A	J	W	T	X
C	J	H	C	L	X	K	V	D	D	F	W	J	E	S	R
P	O	G	C	B	K	W	I	F	E	H	F	V	C	S	F
E	M	A	R	R	I	E	D	T	O	W	G	L	K	M	L

② **Find the family words.**

1. She is the sister of your mother.
2. He is the brother of your mother.
3. He is the dad of your dad.
4. She is the mother of your mother.
5. Your mother and your father are your …
6. She is the daughter of your grandmother.
7. He is the son of your grandmother.
8. She is the daughter of your mum's sister.
9. She is the new wife of your dad.
10. You are not the child, but the … of your granddad.
11. You are the … or
12. … of your uncle.
13. You are the … of your parents.
14. You can have a sister or a ...
15. The new husband of your mother is your …
16. You are the daughter or the … of your parents.

③ **Find the word pairs and colour them.**

mother	aunt	sister	father	brother	uncle
grandma	married	niece	granddad	nephew	divorced

④ **Read the texts and answer the questions.**

This is Liz's family.

Hi, I am Liz and this is my family: my parents, Latisha and Michael, and my brother Dan. My mother works in a hospital and my father works in a big supermarket. He is the manager. My brother is 11 years old. We have a big house in London and we have a dog. His name is Sharky. Our dog loves playing outside in the garden. My mum always tells me to keep my room tidy, especially when granddad and grandmother come to visit us. They live near London. But they don't have a big house.

1. Has Liz got a brother or a sister? Liz has got a ______________________________

2. Where does she live with her family? She lives ______________________________

3. What's the name of her father? Her father's name is ______________________________

4. How old is her brother? He is ______________________________

5. Does Liz have a cat or a dog? She has got a ______________________________

family words 3

This is Lisa's family.

Hi, I am Lisa and I am twelve years old. This is my family. My mum and dad are divorced. I live with my mother in a small flat in Bristol, but I have my own room. My mother's name is Susan. My father's name is Daniel. I have no brother and no sister. We always have fun together. I have a little cat. Her name is Pitty. She loves to sleep in my bed and she always wakes me up. My mother works in the book shop of my uncle. My aunt has no time to help him, because she must take care of my little cousins. They are still babies.

1. Where does Lisa live? ______________________
2. How old is Lisa? ______________________
3. Does she live in a house? ______________________
4. Where does her cat sleep? ______________________
5. Where does her mother work? ______________________

⑤ **Bring a picture or draw your family. Write about your family.**

This is my family.

____

____

____

family tree 1

Look at Susan's family tree and complete the sentences.
Schau dir Susans Familienstammbaum an und ergänze die fehlenden Wörter.

Susan's family tree

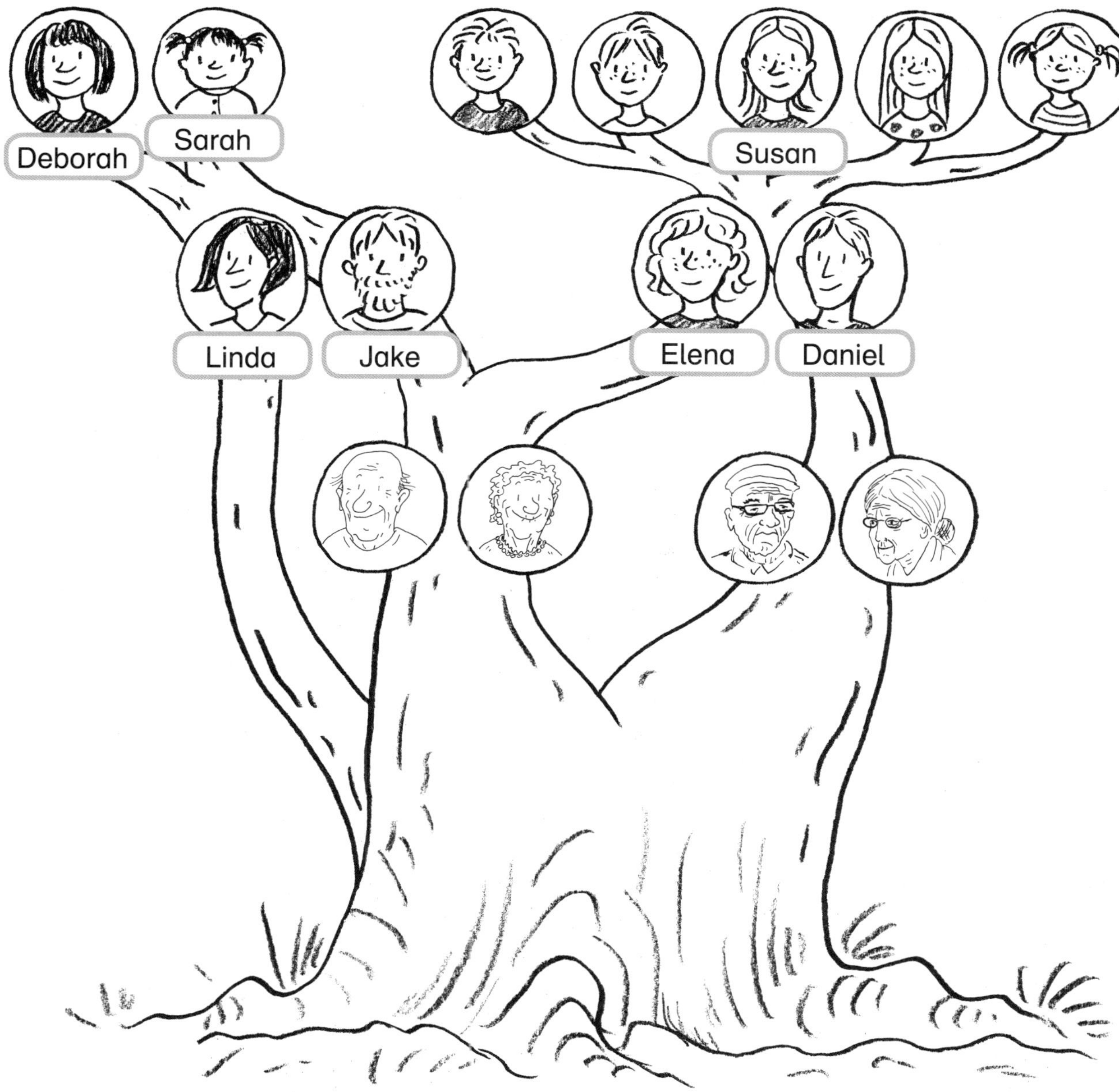

This is Susan's family ________________ (Familienstammbaum). She has got a big family. Her ________________ (Eltern) are Daniel and Elena. She has got two ________________ (Schwestern) and two brothers. Jake is her ________________ (Onkel). He is married to Linda. So Liza has two ________________ (Cousinen), Sarah and Deborah. Her ________________ (Groβvater) is very old. But they have lots of fun together. Her ________________ (Groβmutter) makes the best chocolate cake in town.

family tree 2

2 Make a family tree of your family. The text of exercise 1 might help you!
Zeichne deinen Familienstammbaum. Der Text von Aufgabe 1 (S. 15) kann dir dabei helfen.

Your family tree

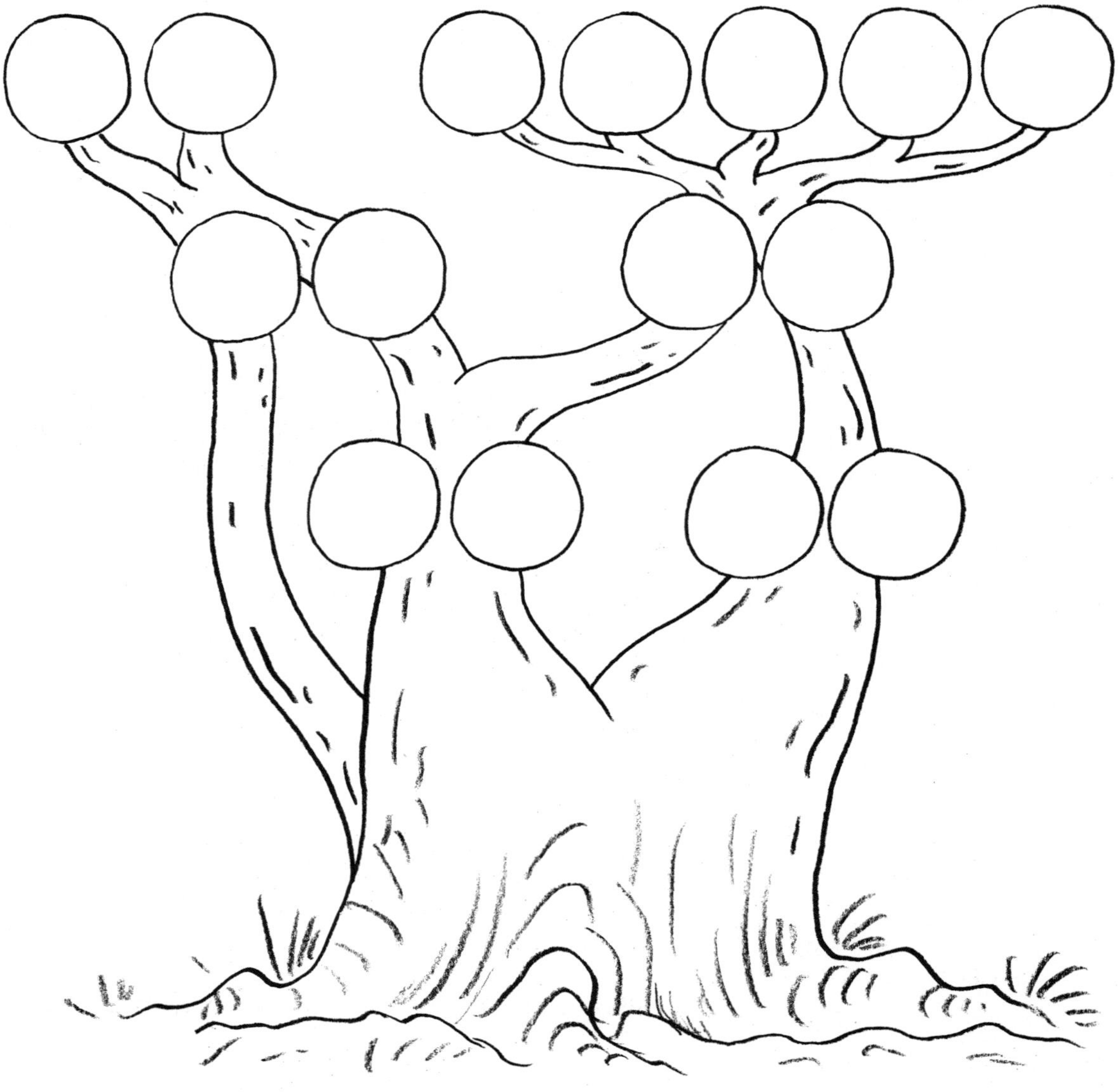

3 Who is your brother? Look at your family tree and complete the sentences.
Schau dir deinen Familienstammbaum an und ergänze die Sätze.

1. My mother's name is ____________________.
2. My father's name is ____________________.
3. I have __________ sisters and __________ brothers.
4. The name of my brother / brothers is / are ____________________.
5. ____________________ is / are my sister / sisters.
6. ____________________ is / are my cousin / cousins.

family tree

① **Look at Susan's family tree and complete the sentences.**

Susan's family tree

This is Susan's family ________________. She has got a big family.

Her ________________ are Daniel and Elena. She has got two ________________

and two brothers. Jake is her ________________. He is married to Linda.

So Liza has two ________________, Sarah and Deborah. Her ________________

is very old. But they have a lot of fun together. Her ________________ makes the best

chocolate cake in town.

② **Make a family tree of your family on an extra sheet of paper. The text of exercise 1 might help you.**

③ **Look at your family tree and write sentences about your family under the picture or on an extra sheet of paper. Who is your brother, what's the name of your mother? Write at least six sentences.**

2 rooms in a house - Übersichtsseite

in the living room (im Wohnzimmer)

sofa (Sofa)

armchair (Sessel)

table (Tisch)

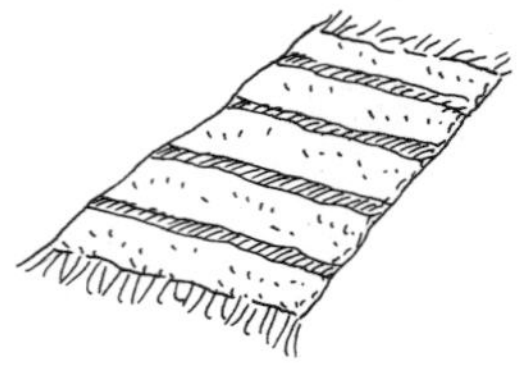
carpet (Teppich)

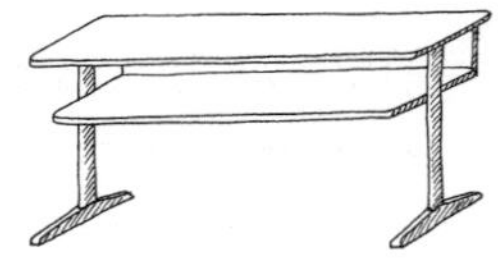
desk (Schreibtisch)

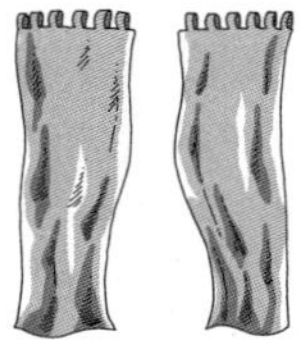
curtains (Vorhänge)

shelf (Regal)

in the bedroom (im Schlafzimmer)

wardrobe (Kleiderschrank)

bed (Bett)

lamp (Lampe)

in the bathroom (im Badezimmer)

shower (Dusche)

sink (Waschbecken)

washing machine (Waschmaschine)

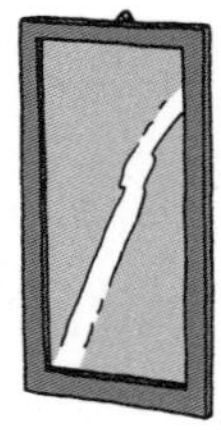
mirror (Spiegel)

toilet (Toilette)

in the kitchen (in der Küche)

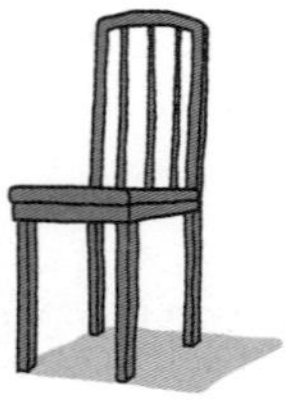
chair (Stuhl)

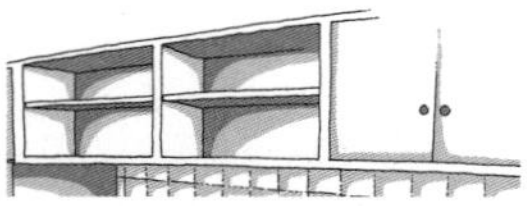
cupboard (Schrank)

dishwasher (Geschirrspülmaschine)

stove (Herd)

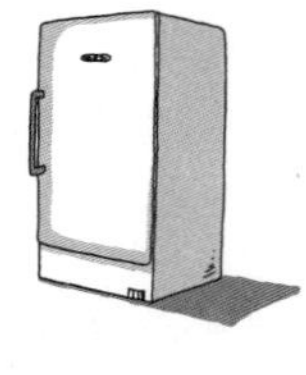
fridge (Kühlschrank)

2 rooms in a house 1

1 Where is Susan's mobile?
Answer the questions. You can use the ideas in the box.

Wo ist Susans Handy? Beantworte die Fragen. Du kannst die Ideen in der Box verwenden.

1. Where is Susan's mobile?  *Susan's mobile is under the bed.*

2. Where is Susan's T-shirt? (auf dem Tisch)  ______________________

3. Where is Susan's school bag? (im Schrank)  ______________________

4. Where are Susan's books? (auf dem Regal)  ______________________

5. Where are Susan's CDs? (unter dem Sofa)  ______________________

6. Where are Susan's felt tips? (auf dem Bett)  ______________________

on the table | in the cupboard | on the shelf | under the sofa | on the bed

2 Name the rooms in the house. Look at the box.
Benenne die Räume in einem Haus. Schau in der Box nach.

______________________  ______________________

______________________ ______________________

bathroom | kitchen | living room | bedroom

2 rooms in a house 2

3 our house

What can you see in the house? Match the parts of the sentences.

Was kannst du in diesem Haus sehen? Verbinde die Satzteile.

1. In the bathroom there is	a) a sofa, a shelf, a TV and a lamp.
2. In the living room there is	b) a bed, a wardrobe, a desk and a chair.
3. In the bedroom there is	c) a shower, a sink and a mirror.
4. In the kitchen there is	d) a cooker, a cupboard, a sink and a dishwasher.

4 Draw your dream room and name all things in it. You can use the ideas in the box.

Zeichne dein Traumzimmer und benenne alle Dinge darin. Du kannst die Ideen in der Box verwenden.

table chair bed wardrobe lamp poster sofa TV CD player
carpet shelf computer

2 rooms in a house 3

5 Read the texts and decide which text belongs to the picture.
Lies die beiden Texte und entscheide, welcher zu dem Bild passt.

a) My house is very big. There are five rooms on the first floor and two rooms on the second. My room is on the second floor. I have two windows and I can see our garden. There's a cupboard in my room. My books are on the desk and my bag is next to the door. There is a TV in my room. My cat always sleeps near my bed.

b) My house is very big. There are five rooms on the first floor and two rooms on the second. My room is on the second floor. I have two windows and I can see our garden. There's a cupboard in my room. My books are on the desk and my bag is next to the door. There is a TV in my room. My dog always sleeps near my bed.

Text ________ belongs to the picture.

6 In the classroom

a) circle *there is* (green) / *there are* (yellow).
Kreise *there is* (grün) und *there are* (gelb) ein.

There are twenty-five students in the classroom and there are twenty-five English books. On the wall there is a poster with our pictures. There are bags next to the tables and there are sandwiches on the desks. There is the teacher's bag next to the board. There are so many pictures on the shelves.

b) What's in your classroom? Write down six words.

Was befindet sich in deinem Klassenraum? Notiere sechs Wörter.

7 Look at the pictures and answer the questions. Tick yes or no.
Schau dir die Bilder an und beantworte die Fragen. Kreuze ja oder nein an.

Sarah's room

Tom's room

1. Is there a cupboard in Sarah's room? ☐ Yes, there is. ☐ No, there isn't.
2. Are there books in the Tom's shelf? ☐ Yes, there are. ☐ No, there aren't.
3. Is there a window in Sarah's room? ☐ Yes, there is. ☐ No, there isn't.
4. Are there posters on Tom's wall? ☐ Yes, there are. ☐ No, there aren't.
5. Are there two doors in Sarah's room? ☐ Yes, there are. ☐ No, there aren't.
6. Are there apples on Tom's bed? ☐ Yes, there are. ☐ No, there aren't.

rooms in a house 5

8 Ask your partner about his room! Write down four things that he has in his room.
Befrage deinen Nachbarn über sein Zimmer und notiere vier Dinge, die in seinem Zimmer sind.

1. Is there a desk in your room?
2. Are there posters in your room?
3. Is there a bed in your room?
4. Are there books in your room?
5. Are there chairs in your room?
6. Is there a wardrobe in your room?
7. Is there a computer in your room?
8. Are there flowers in your room?

1. ____
2. ____
3. ____
4. ____

9 What can you see? Tick the right sentences.
Was siehst du? Kreuze die richtigen Sätze an.

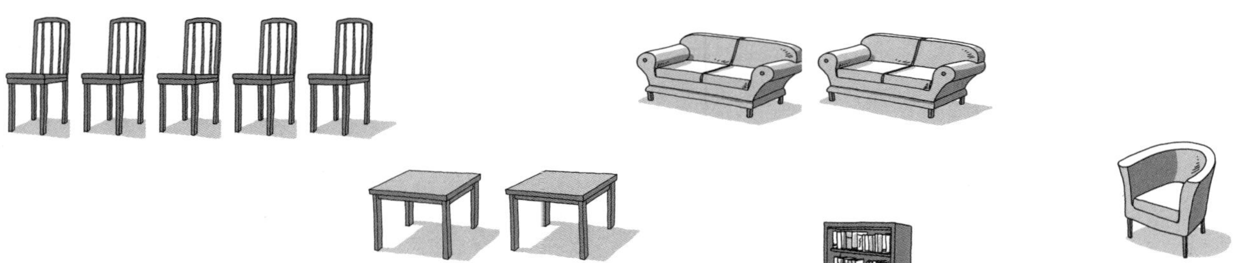

1. There are books. ☐
2. There are five chairs. ☐
3. There are two sofas. ☐
4. There is a poster. ☐
5. There is a wardrobe. ☐
6. There is a cat. ☐
7. There are apples. ☐
8. There is a bed. ☐
9. There are two tables. ☐
10. There is a door. ☐

2 rooms in a house 1

① **Where is Susan's mobile? Answer the questions and use**

on in under

1. Where is Susan's mobile? *Susan's mobile is under the bed.*
2. Where is Susan's T-shirt? (auf dem Tisch) ______
3. Where is Susan's school bag? (im Schrank) ______
4. Where are Susan's books? (auf dem Regal) ______
5. Where are Susan's CDs? (unter dem Sofa) ______
6. Where are Susan's felt tips? (auf dem Bett) ______

② **Name the rooms in the house.**

1.

2.

3.

4.

1. ______
2. ______
3. ______
4. ______

rooms in a house 2

③ **our house**

What can you see in the house? Find four things in each room and write sentences. Use *there is* or *there are*.

1. In the bathroom there is a shower, a sink, a shelf and a ____________________
2. In the ____
3. In the ____
4. In the ____

④ **Draw your dream room on an extra sheet of paper and name all things in it.**

⑤ **Write six sentences about your dream room.**

1. In my dream room **there is** one bed.
2. In my dream room **there are** two chairs.
3. ____
4. ____
5. ____
6. ____

2 rooms in a house 3

(6) **Write about your home on an extra sheet of paper. What's in the rooms? Name three things for each room. Use *there is* or *there are*.**

(7) **Read the texts and decide which text belongs to the picture.**

a) My house is very big. There are five rooms on the first floor and two rooms on the second. My room is on the second floor. I have two windows and I can see our garden. There's a cupboard in my room. My books are on the desk and my bag is next to the door. There is a TV in my room. My cat always sleeps near my bed.

b) My house is very big. There are five rooms on the first floor and two rooms on the second. My room is on the second floor. I have two windows and I can see our garden. There's a cupboard in my room. My books are on the desk and my bag is next to the door. There is a TV in my room. My dog always sleeps near my bed.

c) My house is very big. There are five rooms on the first floor and two rooms on the second. My room is on the second floor. I have three windows and I can see our garden. There's a cupboard in my room. My books are on the desk and my bag is next to the door. There is a TV in my room. My cat always sleeps near my bed.

Text ________ belongs to the picture.

rooms in a house 4

⑧ **Fill in *there is / there are*.**

a) our classroom

__________________ twenty-five students in the classroom and __________________ twenty-five English books. On the wall __________________ a poster with our pictures. __________________ bags next to the tables and __________________ sandwiches on the desks. __________________ the teacher's bag next to the board. __________________ so many books on the shelves.

b) What's in your classroom? Write a short text (4–6 sentences).

____

____

____

____

⑨ **Look at the pictures and answer the questions.**
Use *there is / there are* or *there isn't / there aren't*.

Sarah's room

Tom's room

1. Is there a cupboard in Sarah's room? __________________
2. Are there books in Tom's shelf? __________________
3. Is there a window in Sarah's room? __________________
4. Are there posters on Tom's wall? __________________
5. Are there two doors in Sarah's room? __________________
6. Are there apples on Tom's bed? __________________

rooms in a house 5

⑩ **What can you see? Write eight sentences. Use *there is / there are.***

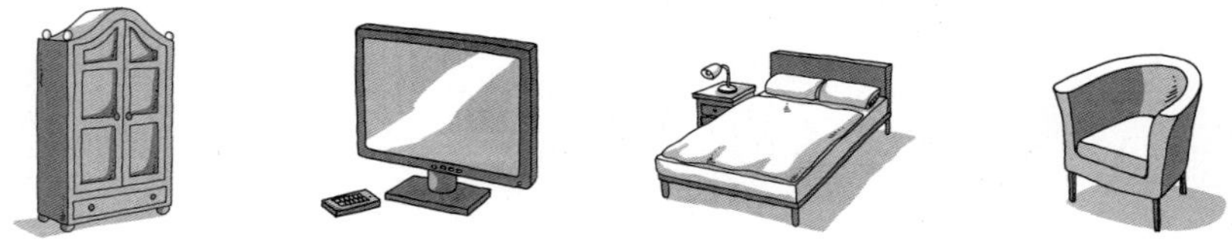

1. There are five chairs.

⑪ **Make a word star and write down the words you know.**

3 my school - Übersichtsseite

classroom phrases

1. Good morning. (Guten Morgen.) 
2. Can I go to the toilet, please? (Darf ich bitte auf die Toilette gehen?) 
3. You're welcome. (Gern geschehen.) 
4. Thank you. (Ich danke dir.) 
5. Sit down, please. (Setz' dich, bitte.) 
6. Open the window, please. (Öffne bitte das Fenster.) 
7. Open your book at page… (Öffnet eure Bücher auf Seite …) 
8. Be quiet, please. (Sei bitte leise.) 
9. Don't talk! (Nicht reden!) / Stop talking! (Hör[t] auf zu sprechen!) 
10. Listen! (Höre zu!) 

subjects

Biology (Biologie)
Chemistry (Chemie)
Physics (Physik)
Religious Education (RE) (Religion)
Social Studies (Gesellschaftslehre)
English (Englisch)
French (Französisch)
Art Education (Kunst)
German (Deutsch)
History (Geschichte)
Technology (Technik)
Maths (Mathe)
Geography (Erdkunde)
Music (Musik)
Physical Education (PE) (Sport)

school things

pencil case (Etui) 
rubber (Radiergummi) 
felt tip (Filzstift) 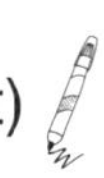
pen (Füller) 
pencil (Bleistift) 
school bag (Schultasche) 
ruler (Lineal) 
pencil sharpener (Anspitzer) 
book (Buch) 
exercise book (Arbeitsheft) 

3 subjects 1

1 Find the words. Look at the box.
Finde die Wörter. Schau in der Box nach.

U	V	H	S	P	H	V	C	X	G	N	X	W	V	I	V	C	I	S	T	D	Y
S	G	E	O	G	R	A	P	H	Y	C	T	B	M	Q	R	P	Q	H	O	J	N
I	E	L	G	A	V	D	W	J	G	C	H	E	M	I	S	T	R	Y	R	S	O
O	L	Z	C	K	M	N	E	O	P	W	H	X	C	P	A	H	K	U	M	D	L
K	F	D	C	W	X	B	I	O	L	O	G	Y	G	M	A	T	H	S	K	A	J
P	N	P	H	Y	S	I	C	S	I	R	X	M	D	P	K	J	U	R	V	D	P
H	O	G	D	C	R	G	E	R	M	A	N	R	I	H	U	X	B	Z	N	V	X
G	Y	U	O	H	O	X	H	L	P	P	W	I	D	Y	S	N	W	S	P	C	K
N	S	O	C	I	A	L	S	T	U	D	I	E	S	S	E	F	R	E	N	C	H
W	H	B	J	H	I	H	U	C	J	E	H	W	X	I	G	Y	P	M	Z	H	D
Y	I	Y	W	X	J	C	W	D	D	I	Z	X	B	C	L	G	X	C	B	I	U
Z	O	F	O	P	Z	I	Y	Y	P	Y	L	Y	M	A	V	W	E	B	B	S	C
L	W	U	Y	G	N	U	T	X	W	R	B	N	N	L	P	E	B	M	Q	T	S
H	Y	A	L	P	T	F	D	H	K	V	D	M	B	E	H	S	U	W	B	O	F
J	F	D	O	G	L	W	M	S	U	O	H	L	T	D	I	M	U	O	G	R	D
Q	P	I	U	U	N	L	G	V	N	Q	T	J	X	U	V	U	C	F	E	Y	Y
L	J	W	S	R	W	H	O	D	E	O	L	Y	V	C	A	S	Z	N	N	X	X
C	R	E	L	I	G	I	O	U	S	E	D	U	C	A	T	I	O	N	G	F	Z
X	F	B	E	F	O	E	Q	F	D	F	P	L	Y	T	C	C	B	V	L	Q	W
H	F	E	A	I	V	R	K	I	M	X	Q	V	I	I	F	M	M	E	I	R	D
W	L	Q	I	H	V	Y	K	C	G	H	G	H	P	O	U	B	G	T	S	P	H
D	T	E	C	H	N	O	L	O	G	Y	E	U	X	N	V	S	S	P	H	J	S

Religious Education, Physical Education, Geography, English, French, Maths, Social studies, Chemistry, Physics, German, Biology

3 subjects 2

2 Look at the timetable and answer the questions.
Schaue in den Stundenplan und beantworte die Fragen.

Sarah's timetable

Monday	Tuesday	Wednesday	Thursday	Friday
English	English	Maths	Art Education	PE
Music	Art Education	Social Studies	German	English
Biology	German	PE	French	German
RE	Maths	Physics	Art Education	Maths
lunch break	Biology	*lunch break*	*lunch break*	History
PE		French	Maths	
Art Education		English	Physics	
		German		
		Maths		

1. What's the first lesson on Monday? Was ist die erste Stunde am Montag?
   It's English.

2. What's the lesson after the lunch break on Monday? Welche Stunde findet am Montag nach der Mittagspause statt?

   It's ____________________________

3. What's lesson 2 on Tuesday? Was ist die zweite Stunde am Dienstag?

   It's ____________________________

4. What's the last lesson on Tuesday? Welches ist die letzte Stunde am Dienstag?

   It's ____________________________

5. What's lesson 3 on Wednesday? Welches ist die dritte Stunde am Mittwoch?

   It's ____________________________

6. What's the lesson after the lunch break on Wednesday?
   Welche Stunde findet mittwochs nach der Mittagspause statt?

   It's ____________________________

7. What's the 2nd lesson on Thursday? Welches ist die zweite Stunde am Donnerstag?

   It's ____________________________

8. What's the lesson after the lunch break on Thursday?
   Welche Stunde findet donnerstags nach der Mittagspause statt?

   It's ____________________________

9. What's the last lesson on Friday? Welches ist die letzte Stunde am Freitag?

   It's ____________________________

3 subjects

① **Find the words.**

W	J	F	D	F	R	T	F	D	X	A	T	H	F	C	R	B	O
F	G	K	D	E	N	W	G	G	O	C	S	B	U	F	E	F	C
M	F	R	E	N	C	H	J	I	Q	B	K	K	G	G	L	I	O
D	J	H	B	F	P	X	Q	G	M	L	Z	I	T	U	I	F	T
S	E	O	D	E	J	W	G	S	E	T	E	A	C	C	G	G	S
A	P	H	Y	S	I	C	A	L	E	D	U	C	A	T	I	O	N
R	T	I	D	L	P	V	E	A	B	M	Y	D	P	V	O	R	P
G	V	D	C	T	N	W	B	R	K	Y	G	H	Z	U	U	P	F
A	N	P	E	P	X	M	G	P	K	I	E	J	P	H	S	T	O
G	M	D	A	T	G	P	E	I	L	R	O	D	W	W	E	O	G
R	X	F	E	T	A	E	N	N	D	D	G	F	W	E	D	Y	K
A	J	F	I	J	O	T	G	C	U	M	R	V	C	V	U	P	T
T	F	T	P	E	V	K	L	M	E	G	A	T	K	M	C	B	W
G	Y	R	S	L	M	I	I	D	K	A	P	R	F	J	A	A	Q
Y	R	S	Y	J	C	T	S	S	G	R	H	R	C	W	T	L	E
S	I	P	G	K	C	U	H	I	P	W	Y	C	I	V	I	B	P
S	J	D	O	Q	M	I	H	B	L	E	K	F	J	C	O	D	W
B	A	J	H	O	S	W	F	R	J	M	F	C	C	D	N	X	G

T	E	V	D	X	M	S	Y	Q	M	W	O	A
B	K	V	E	Y	C	O	Z	U	D	Y	J	C
D	E	R	G	M	P	C	T	F	H	V	K	D
M	B	A	L	X	H	I	X	R	C	B	E	Z
S	Y	F	V	X	Y	A	J	P	H	P	Z	I
T	O	O	B	P	S	L	C	F	E	Y	F	X
H	R	B	Q	R	I	S	Y	G	M	Q	E	A
H	D	Z	R	W	C	T	R	C	I	H	M	Q
U	L	M	B	R	S	U	X	P	S	Q	A	O
W	W	Q	S	G	E	D	B	T	T	K	T	I
G	E	R	M	A	N	I	G	R	R	Y	H	T
Y	Q	I	O	U	Y	E	L	L	Y	T	S	G
H	Y	U	J	G	D	S	M	C	N	M	P	O

② **Look at the timetable and answer the questions.**

Sarah's timetable

Monday	Tuesday	Wednesday	Thursday	Friday
English	English	Maths	Art Education	PE
Music	Art Education	Social Studies	German	English
Biology	German	PE	French	German
RE	Maths	Physics	Art Education	Maths
lunch break	Biology	*lunch break*	*lunch break*	History
PE		French	Maths	
Art Education		English	Physics	
		German		
		Maths		

1. What's the first lesson on Monday? It's ____________________
2. What's the lesson after the lunch break on Monday? ____________________
3. What's lesson 2 on Tuesday? ____________________
4. What's the last lesson on Tuesday? ____________________
5. What's lesson 3 on Wednesday? ____________________
6. What's the lesson after the lunch break on Wednesday? ____________________
7. What's the 2nd lesson on Thursday? ____________________
8. What's the lesson after the lunch break on Thursday? ____________________
9. What's the last lesson on Friday? ____________________

3 school things 1

1 Colour the pairs and write them down.
Male jedes Wortpaar in einer Farbe an. Schreibe es dann auf.

school	stick
school bag	
pencil	tip
glue	bag
exercise	sharpener
felt	case
pencil	book

2 What's in your school bag? Draw six things and write them down in English and German. Look at the box.
Was ist in deiner Schultasche? Zeichne 6 Dinge und schreibe sie auf Englisch und Deutsch auf. Schaue in der Box nach.

ruler

~~ruler~~, pencil case, pencil sharpener, pen, pencil, rubber, felt tips, books, exercise books

3

school things 2

3 Find the words.
Finde die Wörter.

book, exercise book, felt tip, pencil case, school bag, pencil sharpener, pen, pencil, rubber, ruler

4 Read the texts and match them to the pictures. Draw lines.
Lies die Texte und ordne die Kästen zu. Zeichne Linien.

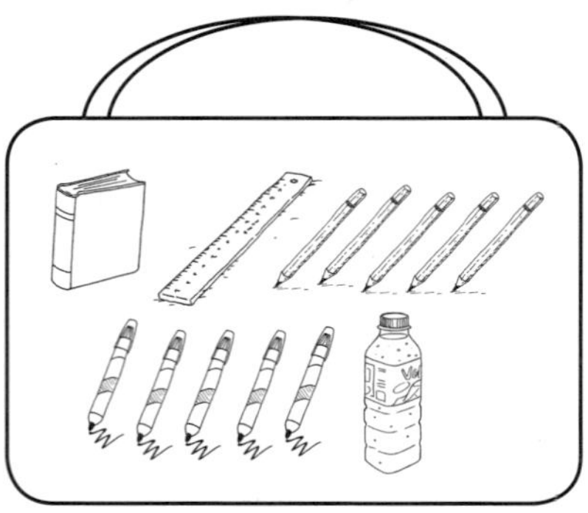

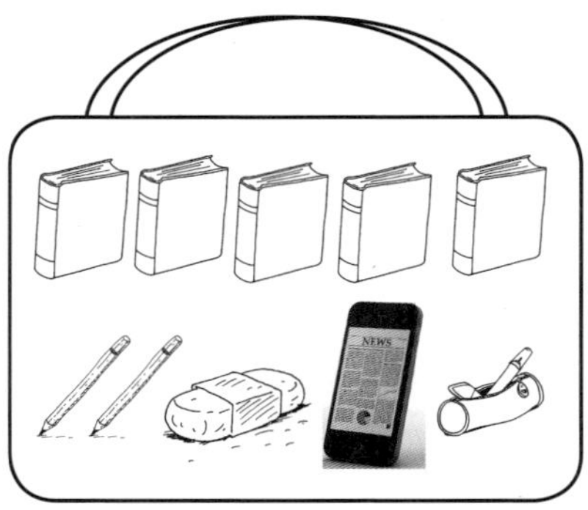

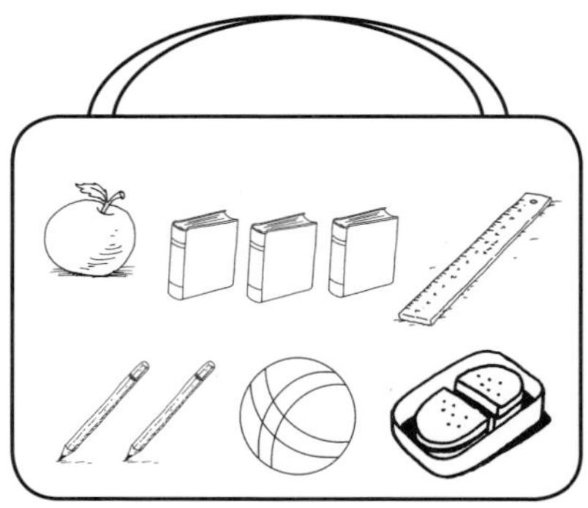

Daniel's bag

In Daniel's bag I can see an apple. He has two pencils and three books. There is a ruler and a sandwich box and a very small ball.

Susan's bag

In Susan's bag there is a book and a ruler. There are many pencils and many felt tips. There is a bottle of water.

teacher's bag

In this bag I can see five books. There are two pencils and there is one rubber and one pencil case. There is a mobile.

3 school things 3

5 What's on your neighbour's desk? Answer the questions and tick the right answer.
Was befindet sich auf dem Tisch deines Nachbarn? Beantworte die Fragen und setze ein Häkchen.

	yes	no
1. Is there a book?		
2. Are there pencils?		
3. Is there a pencil case?		
4. Is there an apple?		
5. Are there exercise books?		
6. Is there a bottle?		

6 What's in your bag? Answer the questions and tick the right answer.
Was hast du dabei? Beantworte die Fragen und setze ein Häkchen.

	yes	no
1. Do you have a bottle of water in your bag?		
2. Do you have sandwiches in your bag?		
3. Is there an English book in your bag?		
4. Do you have a ruler in your pencil case?		

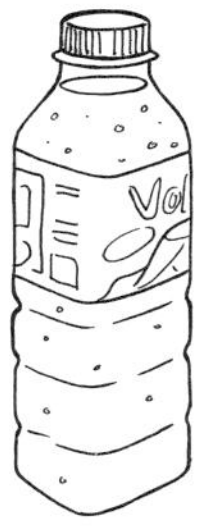

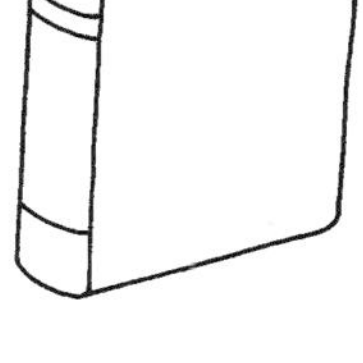

3 at school 1

Read the text and tick the right answer.
Lies den Text und kreuze die richtige Antwort an.

My magic bag

I am Peter and I am a young magician (Zauberer). When I go to school, nothing is in my school bag. But when I sit in the classroom I have all my materials with me. I have a pencil case with all pencils, a rubber and a ruler. And of course I have all the books that I need. After school I go home. I don't take my materials with me and so my bag is easy to carry. Sometimes we have a lot of homework and then I say "Hex Hex – Simsalabim – Abracadabra" and all my materials are with me in my room and I start my homework. Of course it is not me who writes the homework. I am a cool magician.

	right	wrong
1. Peter has nothing in his school bag when he goes to school.		
2. He always has all the materials he needs.		
3. He takes the materials with him when he goes home.		
4. He says "welcome to my class", when he is at home.		
5. He does his homework by himself.		
6. Peter is an old magician.		
7. He has a pencil sharpener in his pencil case.		
8. After school he plays football.		

Emma's email

Read Emma's email to her friend in London about her new school. Read the questions and tick the right answer.

Emma schreibt ihrer Freundin in London eine E-Mail über die neue Schule. Lies die E-Mail und kreuze die richtige Antwort an.

Hi Sandra,

My new school is very nice. We have a big classroom. There are nice posters on the wall.

All the pupils are nice and my teacher is nice, too. My new friends always make funny jokes.

We are in the same tutor group. After school we do homework together and then we play football. I am not very good at football but David shows me all the tricks. We always have a lot of fun together.

See you, Emma

	right	wrong
Emma's new school is boring.		
The classroom is big.		
The pupils aren't nice.		
Her new friends make funny jokes.		
They aren't in the same tutor group.		
After school they do homework.		
Emma is good at football.		

3 at school 3

3 Think about your school and describe it. Tick the right answer. You can add more ideas.

Denke an deine Schule und beschreibe sie. Kreuze die richtige Antwort an. Sollte dir noch etwas einfallen, kannst du es ergänzen.

	right	wrong
My school is big.		
My teacher is nice.		
My classroom is small.		
There are many posters on the wall.		
There are nice pupils in my class.		
We play at the playground together.		

4 Match the pictures to the text. Take care of the underlined words.

Verbinde die Texte mit den Bildern. Achte dabei auf die unterstrichenen Wörter.

This is my new school. It is very big. We have many classrooms and a nice playground.

I love the cafeteria. There I can eat sandwiches and crisps with my friends. We have fun together and relax.

In the classroom are all my books. We leave the bags there. We have nice posters on the wall and all the books are on the table.

This is our gym. It is so big and we have many balls. We love sports. Our teacher often plays basketball with us.

The caretaker has his own room. He has all the materials there.

Nadja Brize, Amel Selmi: Wortschatz 5. Klasse – Inklusionsmaterial

3 at school 4

5 Make word stars and use the words in the chart. You can also use your own ideas.
Bilde Wortsterne, indem du die Wörter aus der Tabelle ergänzt. Streiche diese durch. Fallen dir noch weitere ein? Ergänze die Tabelle.

board	bag	~~ruler~~	table	chair	pencil	teacher	sandwich
book	~~computer~~	pupil	felt tip	rubber	cafeteria	caretaker	poster
play-ground	window	~~wall~~	door				

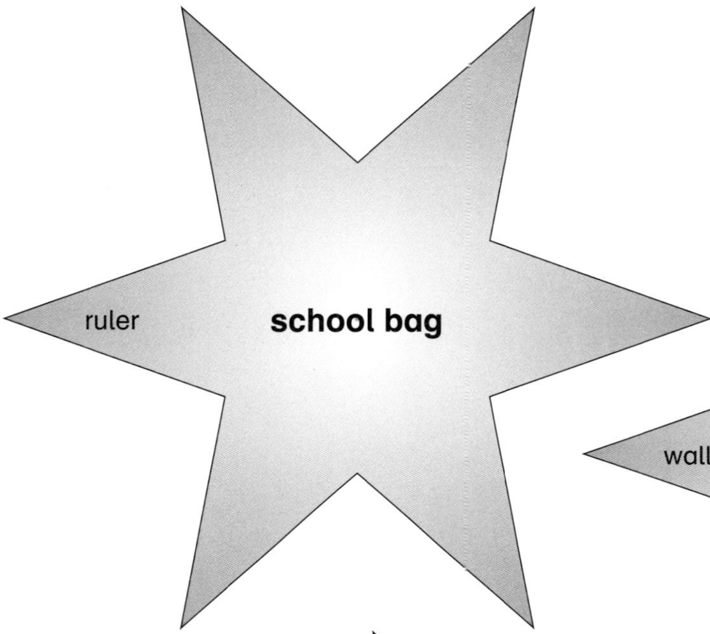

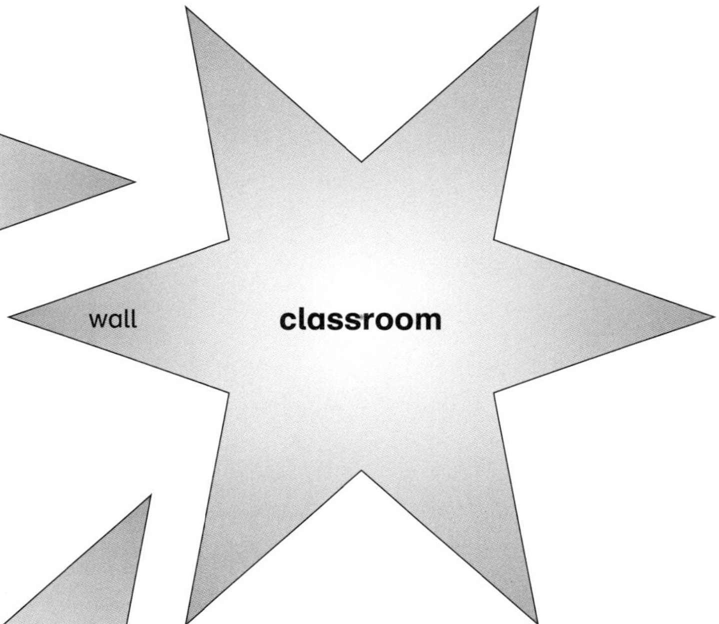

3 school things 1

① **school things – match the parts of the words and write the words down.**

glue | exercise | felt | pencil | bag | case | stick | book | school | tip | sharpener

② **What's in your school bag? Draw six things and write them down in English and German.**

ruler – Lineal

③ **Find the words.**

1. 
2. 
3. 
4. 
5. 

6. 
7. 
8. 
9. 
10. 

school things 2

④ **What's in the pupil's bags?**

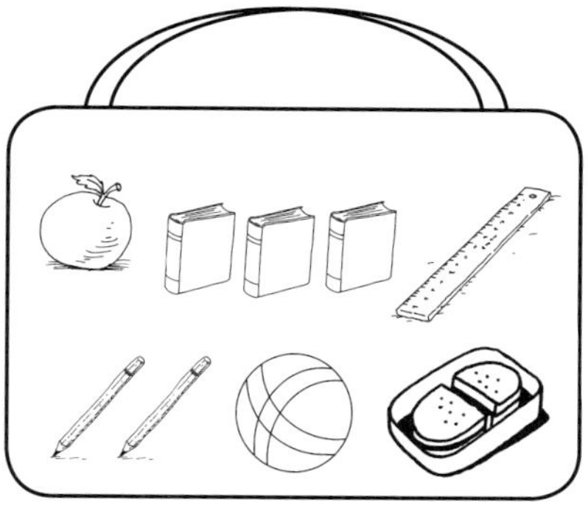

In Daniel's bag I can see *an apple*, ______

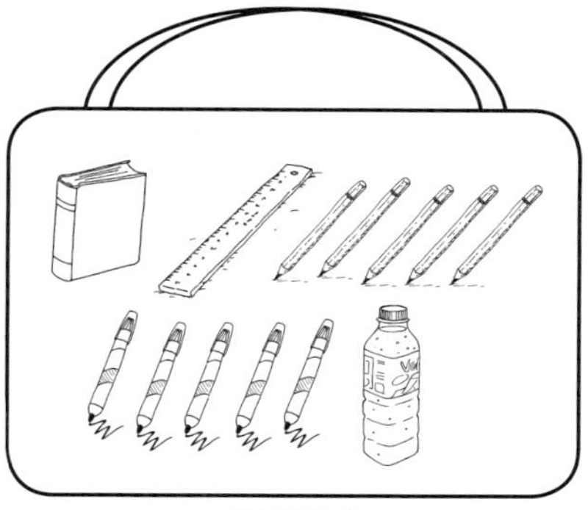

In Susan's bag I can see ______

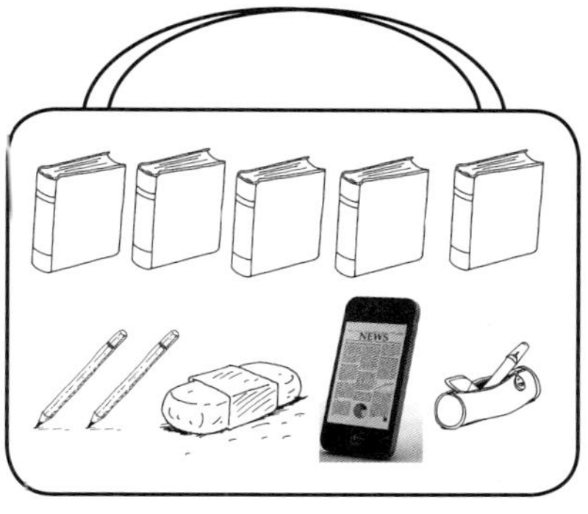

In the teachers's bag I can see ______

⑤ **Look at your neighbour's desk and write down six sentences what she / he has got on the desk.**

1. ______
2. ______
3. ______
4. ______
5. ______
6. ______

⑥ **Answer the questions with "Yes, I have." or "No, I haven't.".**

1. Do you have a bottle of water in your bag? ______
2. Do you have sandwiches in your bag? ______
3. Do you have an English book in your bag? ______
4. Do you have a ruler in your pencil case? ______

① **Read the text and answer the questions.**

My magic bag

I am Peter and I am a young magician. When I go to school, nothing is in my school bag. But when I sit in the classroom I have all my materials with me. I have a pencil case with all pencils, a rubber and a ruler. And of course I have all the books that I need. After school I go home. I don't take my materials with me and so my bag is easy to carry. Sometimes we have a lot of homework and then I say "Simsalabim – Abracadabra" and all my materials are with me in my room and I start my homework. Of course it is not me who writes the homework. I am a cool magician.

1. What's in the school bag when Peter goes to school?

____

2. Does he have all the materials at school?

____

3. Does he take the materials with him when he goes home?

____

4. What does he say when he is at home?

____

5. Does he do his homework by himself?

____

② **Read Emma's email to her friend in London and answer the questions.**

Hi Sandra,

My new school is very nice. We have a big classroom. There are nice posters on the wall.

All the pupils are nice and my teacher is nice too. My new friends always make funny jokes.

We are in the same tutor group. After school we do homework together and then we play football. I am not very good at football but David shows me all the tricks. We always have a lot of fun together.

See you, Emma

3 at school 2

1. How is Emma's school? ______________________

2. Is the classroom small? ______________________

3. Are the pupils nice? ______________________

4. Is Emma good at football? ______________________

(3) Write an email to a friend about your school. Use the ideas in the box.

school big / small – teacher – classroom – wall – posters – nice pupils – play – nice class

(4) Match the pictures to the text. Read carefully!

This is my new school. It is very big. We have many classrooms and a nice playground.

I love the cafeteria. There I can eat sandwiches and crisps with my friends. We have fun together and relax.

In the classroom are all my books. We leave the bags there. We have nice posters on the wall and all the books are on the table.

This is our gym. It is so big and we have many balls. We love sports. Our teacher often plays basketball with us.

The caretaker has his own room. He has all the materials there.

5 **Make word stars.**

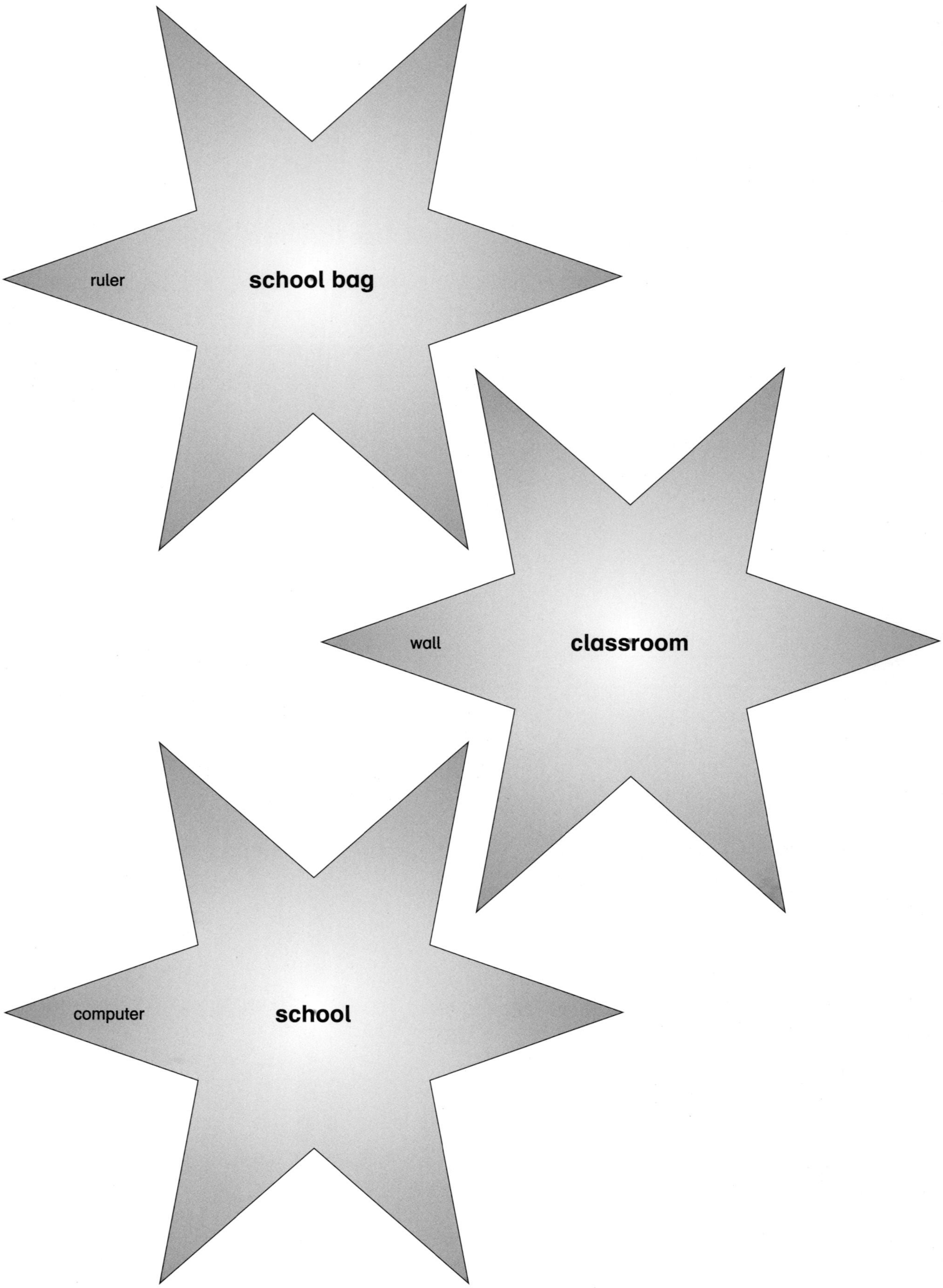

my free time – Übersichtsseite

play football (Fußball spielen)

play basketball (Basketball spielen)

ride a horse (auf einem Pferd reiten)

inline skating (Inliner fahren)

play computer games (Computerspiele spielen)

play the piano (Klavier spielen)

go dancing (tanzen gehen)

read books (Bücher lesen)

sing in a band (in einer Band singen)

do judo / karate (Judo / Karate machen)

collect stamps (Briefmarken sammeln)

cycling / ride a bike (Radfahren)

draw / paint a picture (ein Bild zeichnen / malen)

ice skating (eislaufen)

listen to music (Musik hören)

play tennis (Tennis spielen)

skiing (Skifahren)

swimming (schwimmen)

4 my free time 1

1 What free time activities can Sarah do?
Write down what Sarah can do in her free time and what she can't do.
Sarah hat viele Hobbies. Was kann sie? Was kann sie nicht? Ergänze die Sätze.

1.  ✔  ✗ (play football / play basketball)

Sarah can play football but she can't play basketball.

2.  ✔  ✗ (ride a bike / ride horses)

Sarah can ______________________ but she can't ______________________.

3.  ✔  ✗ (read books / play the piano)

Sarah can ______________________ but she can't ______________________.

4.  ✔  ✗ (paint pictures / sing songs)

____

5.  ✔  ✗ (play computer games / do inline skating)

____

6.  ✔  ✗ (go swimming / go dancing)

____

2 Look at the pictures. What things can you collect? Find the right word for each picture.
Schau dir die Bilder an. Was kannst du sammeln? Finde das richtige Wort für jedes Bild.

You can collect ...

 ______________________  ______________________

 ______________________  ______________________

 ______________________  ______________________

CDs, cards, stamps, T-shirts, comics, books

3 What do you collect? What don't you collect? Tick the right answer. Write down 2 more things you collect / don't collect.

Was sammelst du? Was sammelst du nicht? Kreuze die richtige Antwort an. Schreibe zwei weitere Dinge auf, die du sammelst / nicht sammelst.

I collect ☐ stamps ☐ cards ☐ T-shirts ☐ dolls ☐ CDs ☐ comics ☐ books

I don't collect ☐ stamps ☐ cards ☐ T-shirts ☐ dolls ☐ CDs ☐ comics ☐ books

____

4 What hobbies do you know? Translate.
Welche Hobbies kennst du? Übersetze.

1	Cricket spielen	m	a	cycling / ride a bike
2	reiten	___	b	do judo
3	Rad fahren	___	c	sing in a band
4	inlineskaten	___	d	go dancing
5	Briefmarken sammeln	___	e	watch TV
6	eislaufen	___	f	play the guitar
7	schwimmen gehen	___	g	go shopping
8	Judo	___	h	inline skating
9	Computer spielen	___	i	play computer games
10	Gitarre spielen	___	j	go swimming
11	fernsehen	___	k	collect stamps
12	tanzen	___	l	ride
13	einkaufen gehen	___	m	play cricket
14	in einer Band singen	___	n	ice skating

5 sports at school
What sports do you do at your school? Tick the right answer.

At school we ☐ play football ☐ play basketball ☐ play cricket
☐ do judo ☐ go swimming ☐ go dancing
☐ go riding ☐ play badminton ☐ play table tennis

6 What is Jane doing at the weekend?
Match the pictures to the sentences.
Schau dir die Bilder an und finde die passenden Sätze.

①  a) Janet is watching TV. *picture 5*

②  b) Janet is playing tennis. ____________

③  c) Janet is tidying her room. ____________

④  d) Janet is helping in the garden. ____________

⑤  e) Janet is washing the car. ____________

⑥  f) Janet is playing the guitar. ____________

⑦  g) Janet is reading a book. ____________

⑧  h) Janet is painting a picture. ____________

⑨  i) Janet is doing homework. ____________

⑩  j) Janet is playing with her mobile phone. ____________

7 Find the words. Look at the box.

Finde die Wörter. Schau in der Box nach.

O	J	P	L	A	Y	F	O	O	T	B	A	L	L	M	H	L	A	L	F
S	K	I	W	Y	M	O	G	I	F	I	N	U	M	A	O	C	A	H	Y
E	D	A	N	C	I	N	G	M	Q	L	R	E	A	D	I	N	G	A	Q
A	V	S	Q	J	N	T	S	K	T	C	D	I	R	L	C	E	O	U	Y
I	T	R	J	S	D	P	L	A	Y	B	A	S	K	E	T	B	A	L	L
C	G	B	L	K	U	E	Y	B	S	W	K	N	W	L	H	V	Y	I	K
Y	O	M	I	I	J	V	S	D	R	A	W	I	N	G	B	J	B	V	C
C	G	H	I	I	G	N	L	I	C	V	L	D	B	C	S	G	L	X	J
L	G	X	I	N	K	H	I	N	L	I	N	E	S	K	A	T	I	N	G
I	F	T	O	G	A	W	V	P	P	K	K	O	Q	Q	T	I	X	B	N
N	P	I	T	Q	P	B	R	X	Z	J	E	N	H	X	E	B	J	R	V
G	E	P	L	A	Y	C	O	M	P	U	T	E	R	G	A	M	E	S	B
D	J	Q	Y	Q	K	X	C	D	W	Y	X	E	E	Q	R	M	U	B	B
K	G	D	K	F	H	C	P	L	A	Y	T	H	E	P	I	A	N	O	Q
U	Z	G	I	Z	R	L	I	Z	B	C	Z	H	U	K	R	Y	K	V	T
C	D	H	Q	R	I	D	E	A	H	O	R	S	E	Y	D	L	M	C	I
K	O	Y	L	M	A	I	N	R	J	H	J	K	J	R	R	O	N	T	J
X	S	U	J	L	T	A	B	L	E	T	E	N	N	I	S	V	F	N	X
C	D	Y	S	K	Q	E	H	O	J	Y	Y	P	Y	R	I	X	F	F	B
R	U	C	L	I	M	B	I	N	G	Q	S	W	I	M	M	I	N	G	I

play football
play basketball
ride a horse
inline skating
play computer games
play the piano
dancing
reading
climbing
cycling
drawing
table tennis
skiing
swimming

8 do judo – play football

Write the hobbies in the chart.

Schreibe die Hobbies in die richtige Spalte der Tabelle.

Hobbies:

play table tennis
go shopping
~~play football~~
go riding
do inline skating
play basketball
play badminton
~~go dancing~~
play ice hockey
go swimming
~~do judo~~

do	play	go
do judo	*play football*	*go dancing*

4 my free time 1

① **What free time activities can Sarah do?**

Write down what Sarah can do in her free time and what she can't do.

1.  ✔  ✗

Sarah can play football but she can't play basketball.

2.  ✔  ✗

Sarah can ______________________ but she can't ______________________.

3.  ✔  ✗

____.

4.  ✔  ✗

____

5.  ✔  ✗

____

6.  ✔  ✗

____

② **What things can you collect? Look at the pictures. Write down the words.**

You can collect ...

 ______________________  ______________________

 ______________________  ______________________

 ______________________  ______________________

③ **Do you know the English words? Write them down.**

Cricket spielen ______

inlineskaten ______

Judo ______

eislaufen ______

Rad fahren ______

tanzen ______

Gitarre spielen ______

Briefmarken sammeln ______

in einer Band singen ______

schwimmen gehen ______

einkaufen gehen ______

fernsehen ______

Computer spielen ______

reiten ______

④ **What sports do you do at school? Write down the words.**

At school we ______

______

⑤ **Look at the signs for a playground.**
a) What can you do there?

1. We can play football.
2. We can ______
3. ______
4. ______
5. ______
6. ______
7. ______
8. ______

b) And what can't you do there?

1. We can't ride a bike.
2. We can't ______________________
3. ______________________
4. ______________________
5. ______________________
6. ______________________

⑥ **Look at the pictures and write down what Janet is doing at the weekend.**

○ Janet is watching TV.

○ Janet is tidying ______________________

○ Janet is ______________________

○ ______________________

○ ______________________

○ ______________________

⑦ **Find the words.**

K	R	M	M	G	M	T	N	L	R	R	Q	E	J	V	J	S	M	M	L	E	S	M	Z	O	J	T
N	D	Q	V	C	Y	I	H	G	C	V	J	L	Q	C	P	N	V	N	C	W	T	L	C	C	F	P
Y	X	B	A	U	V	E	V	O	K	J	E	S	B	B	K	Z	Q	X	L	W	Z	O	K	D	M	F
B	P	C	D	X	K	G	I	D	G	M	M	B	G	A	W	U	S	Y	S	K	I	I	N	G	F	C
K	U	I	B	N	H	P	L	A	Y	C	O	M	P	U	T	E	R	G	A	M	E	S	L	Q	D	M
S	G	A	S	S	P	H	B	N	L	Z	C	Z	L	L	S	T	J	O	S	M	C	R	J	F	B	S
L	L	T	W	P	L	K	E	C	Z	G	K	E	S	S	O	G	I	Y	I	G	E	I	V	W	V	U
B	I	W	I	Y	A	I	I	I	O	T	C	E	B	D	S	B	N	V	N	B	F	W	K	P	V	U
K	G	U	M	L	Y	X	O	N	Y	H	U	I	U	Q	V	G	L	K	G	T	O	P	U	W	V	O
N	Q	D	M	Y	B	O	P	G	D	N	B	F	U	U	D	P	I	P	I	I	Q	C	X	P	M	W
U	F	R	I	M	A	V	T	E	F	D	N	T	L	T	W	L	N	P	N	B	R	S	C	M	N	P
C	V	A	N	T	S	F	O	G	Y	W	H	G	G	M	D	A	E	V	A	V	A	L	O	F	D	M
L	S	W	G	P	K	I	C	E	S	K	A	T	I	N	G	Y	S	O	B	C	L	A	L	R	O	C
M	H	A	W	H	E	T	D	Q	U	K	D	K	V	W	W	T	K	P	A	S	D	X	L	I	J	P
E	K	P	O	A	T	D	O	C	H	S	B	X	H	S	R	E	A	X	N	V	M	E	E	D	U	L
V	N	I	A	M	B	A	J	C	D	H	E	S	B	R	Q	N	T	B	D	J	K	J	C	E	D	W
F	T	C	C	Y	A	N	I	G	O	Z	V	Y	O	G	E	N	I	N	K	B	M	Q	T	A	O	I
D	Y	T	F	J	L	H	B	Z	F	V	C	Q	X	X	N	I	N	G	L	N	W	I	T	H	H	K
T	P	U	R	D	L	M	T	P	C	E	Q	I	T	K	C	S	G	W	A	X	X	N	H	O	F	E
Z	Q	R	F	C	L	I	M	B	I	N	G	K	K	J	K	V	V	G	G	V	G	P	I	R	Y	I
N	V	E	F	Y	W	O	A	R	R	E	A	D	B	O	O	K	S	H	T	C	P	X	N	S	N	P
X	V	G	J	L	H	I	U	B	Q	C	Y	C	L	I	N	G	O	J	V	O	L	N	G	E	C	T
J	K	S	S	G	T	N	Z	P	P	L	A	Y	T	H	E	P	I	A	N	O	M	A	S	X	P	W
M	U	E	Q	L	I	S	T	E	N	T	O	M	U	S	I	C	M	B	C	L	R	P	I	Z	G	H
H	P	X	W	Q	G	S	E	M	C	I	C	W	T	P	U	A	U	Q	A	N	M	U	J	W	Q	N
I	R	R	E	F	X	D	F	M	R	O	I	U	Q	Y	S	G	U	Y	Z	O	Y	B	D	J	L	A
Y	T	D	K	V	U	Y	P	L	A	Y	F	O	O	T	B	A	L	L	I	V	V	G	B	G	W	N

- play football
- ride a horse
- play computer games
- go dancing
- sing in a band
- collect things
- draw a picture
- listen to music
- skiing
- do judo
- play basketball
- inline skating
- play the piano
- read books
- climbing
- cycling
- ice skating
- play tennis
- swimming

my free time 5

⑧ do judo – play football

Match *do*, *go*, *play* with the hobbies and write them in the chart.

hobbies:
table tennis
shopping
~~football~~
riding
inline skating
basketball
badminton
dancing
ice hockey
swimming
~~do judo~~

do	play	go
do judo	*play football*	*go dancing*

⑨ What are your hobbies?

Write five sentences about your hobbies. Write down what sports or activities you like, what you don't like, what you do and what you collect.

1. ______________________________
2. ______________________________
3. ______________________________
4. ______________________________
5. ______________________________

⑩ What's Oscar's hobby?

Read the text and answer the questions.

Oscar is 11 years old. He loves sports. Every Monday he goes to the football training. On Saturday he has his first football match. But he is not nervous, because he has new football shoes and a new T-shirt with the number 11. This is his favourite number. He sometimes meets his friends after school. They play football, listen to music or play computer games. But his favourite hobby is football. He watches the matches on TV with his father and they have a lot of fun together.

1. How old is Oscar? ______________________________
2. What does he do on Mondays? ______________________________
3. Does Oscar have a basketball game on Saturday? ______________________________
4. What is his favourite hobby? ______________________________
5. Does Oscar have a new pair of jeans? ______________________________
6. What does Oscar do after school? ______________________________

5 my pets and animals - Übersichtsseite

aquarium (Aquarium)

cage (Käfig)

basket (Korb)

dog (Hund)

cat (Katze)

guinea pig (Meerschweinchen)

hamster (Hamster)

bird (Vogel)

fish (Fisch)

horse (Pferd)

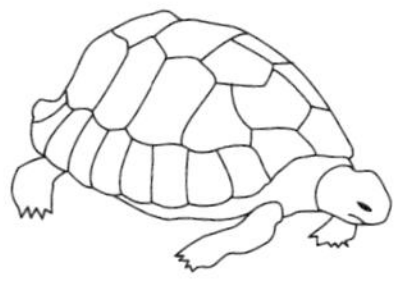
tortoise (Schildkröte)

rabbit (Kaninchen)

parrot (Papagei)

mouse (Maus)

budgie (Wellensittich)

snake (Schlange)

cow (Kuh)

pig (Schwein)

goose (Gans)

sheep (Schaf)

crocodile (Krokodil)

bear (Bär)

giraffe (Giraffe)

monkey (Affe)

zebra (Zebra)

elephant (Elefant)

tiger (Tiger)

5 my pets and animals 1

1 Where do the pets sleep?
Match the words and the pictures and make sentences.
Verbinde die Wörter und die Bilder und schreibe Sätze auf.

basket
cage
aquarium

1. The dog sleeps in a basket.
2. The guinea pig sleeps in a ______________________________
3. The ______________ sleeps in a ______________________
4. The ______________ sleeps in an ______________________
5. The ______________ sleeps in a ______________________
6. The ______________ sleeps in a ______________________

2 What do the pets eat? Complete the sentences. You can use the ideas in the box.
Was essen Haustiere? Vervollständige die Sätze. Du kannst die Ideen in der Box verwenden.

meat  fish  vegetables  salad 
carrots  apples  grass 

1.  Dogs eat meat.
2.  Cats eat ______________________________
3.  Rabbits eat ______________________________
4.  Hamsters eat ______________________________
5.  Horses eat ______________________________
6.  Birds eat ______________________________
7.  Tortoises eat ______________________________

5 my pets and animals 2

3 What do the pets do? Match the words.

cats	play (spielen)
dogs	swim (schwimmen)
birds	sleep (schlafen)
fish	run (rennen)
hamsters	jump (springen)
guinea pigs	fly (fliegen)

4 Find the animals. Finde die Tiere.

X	W	H	A	M	S	T	E	R	L	D	F	R
L	M	Y	T	U	B	T	B	K	Y	N	W	A
E	T	P	S	X	S	L	P	S	Y	G	M	B
S	O	B	X	V	F	I	S	H	M	P	X	B
Q	R	O	A	S	Q	X	T	C	E	A	F	I
A	T	O	K	F	Q	W	L	S	Z	R	S	T
R	O	F	Q	C	W	H	C	E	U	R	U	N
O	I	Q	H	J	B	O	M	B	N	O	I	K
X	S	B	B	I	H	R	S	C	Y	T	K	D
P	E	O	B	A	P	S	W	F	Y	K	I	O
X	Q	E	I	H	U	E	U	M	C	K	C	G
E	O	K	R	P	T	H	D	T	A	H	T	Q
Q	X	G	D	V	U	M	R	C	T	O	Q	L

rabbit
horse
cat
dog
bird
tortoise
hamster
parrot
fish

5 my pets and animals 3

5 Colour the pets.
Male die Tiere in den genannten Farben an.

1. Colour the  blue.
budgie

2. Colour the  brown.
dog

3. Colour the  black.
horse

4. Colour the  green.
parrot

5. Colour the  pink.
rabbit

6. Colour the  yellow.
tortoise

7. Colour the  red.
guinea pig

8. Colour the  purple.
hamster

6 Find the english words.
Finde die englischen Wörter.

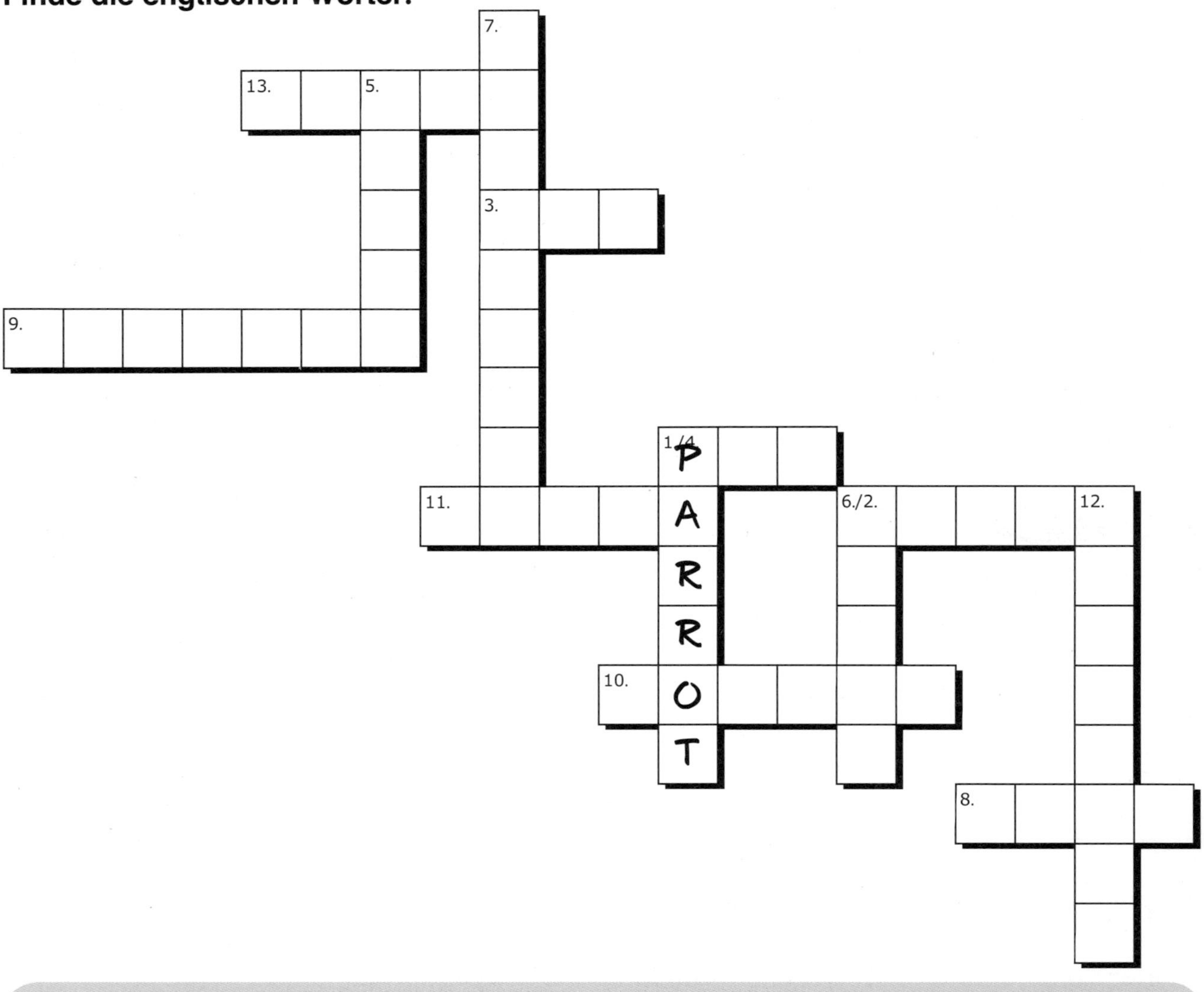

1. Papagei – 2. Schlange – 3. Kuh – 4. Schwein – 5. Gans – 6. Schaf – 7. Krokodil – 8. Bär – 9. Giraffe – 10. Affe – 11. Zebra – 12. Elefant – 13. Tiger

my pets and animals 4

7 Read the text and tick the right answer.
Lies den Text und kreuze die richtige Antwort an.

The class is on a trip to London farm. The pupils are very excited, because it is the first time they visit a farm. The teacher tells them about the animals and pets and about the food. The farm offers special activities for young and old people. They can help the farmer to feed the chicken, pigs, cows and sheep and they can ride horses. But they must be careful. Later they can visit the fields of the farm, have a picnic there and enjoy the nature.

Who has a trip to London farm?	☐ a class	☐ your parents
What does the teacher tell them about?	☐ animals	☐ clothes
What does the farm offer?	☐ special activities	☐ games
Who can visit the farm?	☐ young and old people	☐ teachers
What can the pupils do?	☐ do homework	☐ help the farmer
What can they visit later?	☐ the fields	☐ shops
What can they have?	☐ breakfast	☐ a picnic

8 Complete the sentences and think of suitable words.
Vervollständige die Sätze und überlege dir passende Wörter.

1.  2.  3.  4.  5.  6. 

1. In the living room there is a ________________ in the aquarium.
2. In the garden there is a ________________.
3. The ________________ barks.
4. The ________________ lies on the bed.
5. The ________________ says the same things we say.
6. The ________________ are on the fields and eat grass.

5 my pets and animals 1

① **Where do the pets sleep? Match the words and the pictures and make sentences.**

basket
cage
aquarium

1. The dog sleeps in a basket.
2. ____________________
3. ____________________
4. ____________________
5. ____________________
6. ____________________

② **What do the pets eat? Complete the sentences. You can use the ideas in the box.**

~~meat~~ – fish – vegetables – salad – carrots – apples – grass

1. Dogs eat meat.
2. Cats eat ____________________
3. Rabbits eat ____________________
4. Hamsters eat ____________________
5. Horses eat ____________________
6. Birds eat ____________________
7. Tortoises eat ____________________

③ **What do the pets do? Match the words.**

cats	play
dogs	swim
birds	sleep
fish	run
hamsters	jump
guinea pigs	fly

my pets and animals 2

4 Find the animals and write them down.

J	B	O	M	Y	O	F	U	A	L	K	A	R	D	Y	L	C	E	I
Q	Z	P	K	C	N	H	O	R	S	E	D	L	V	H	B	B	J	H
R	B	J	T	E	B	E	N	L	B	G	E	O	Z	F	M	J	D	R
C	F	L	H	E	C	G	H	D	K	H	D	N	I	Y	G	L	B	Y
P	Z	Z	O	H	P	D	H	M	E	O	L	H	S	W	M	D	Z	D
U	I	B	G	I	R	A	F	F	E	R	P	I	V	T	M	J	S	Z
E	I	V	O	T	E	O	V	C	E	S	H	P	I	G	L	T	P	R
Q	N	V	F	M	H	N	W	D	J	E	B	H	J	H	C	K	B	S
N	D	L	Q	R	D	O	Y	Z	T	X	W	O	S	I	M	X	W	U
I	T	F	E	U	D	V	X	E	M	C	C	H	A	M	S	T	E	R
V	D	G	U	I	V	E	U	I	J	I	U	S	G	V	Q	C	U	U
P	U	P	C	O	W	G	P	R	C	L	I	W	N	Z	Z	A	I	F
Z	U	R	A	B	B	I	T	M	J	R	U	C	I	S	P	T	J	H
U	D	Z	H	F	N	Q	N	P	Z	O	A	E	B	E	A	R	V	O
J	D	X	C	R	O	C	O	D	I	L	E	D	P	E	N	F	T	R
S	O	L	Z	Z	V	X	H	A	L	Y	L	C	L	S	H	C	I	S
Y	G	V	N	J	A	V	M	F	X	X	Y	G	V	H	L	M	G	E
U	G	U	I	N	E	A	P	I	G	Q	S	N	A	K	E	L	E	O
S	H	O	P	M	X	J	O	T	K	W	Y	G	K	A	C	B	R	E

guinea pig

____

____

____

____

5 Colour the pets.

1. Colour the budgie blue. 
2. Colour the dog brown. 
3. Colour the horse black. 
4. Colour the parrot green. 
5. Colour the rabbit pink. 
6. Colour the tortoise yellow. 
7. Colour the guinea pig red. 
8. Colour the hamster purple. 

⑥ **What is it in English? Write it down.**

1. Hund
2. Katze
3. Meerschweinchen
4. Hamster
5. Schildkröte
6. Hase
7. Papagei
8. Wellensittich
9. Kuh
10. Schwein
11. Pferd
12. Zebra
13. Elefant
14. Tiger

⑦ **What kinds of animals live on the farm? What can you see in the zoo?**

Think of animals and pets and write down as many words as you can. The pictures below might help you.

in the zoo	on the farm

(8) **Read the text and answer the questions.**

London farm

The class is on a trip to London farm. The pupils are very excited, because it is the first time they visit a farm. The teacher tells them about the animals and pets and about the food. The farm offers special activities for young and old people. They can help the farmer to feed the chicken, pigs, cows and sheep and they can ride horses. But they must be careful. Later they can visit the fields of the farm, have a picnic there and enjoy the landscape.

1. Who has a trip to London farm? ______________________________
2. What does the teacher tell them about? ______________________________
3. What does the farm offer? ______________________________
4. Who can visit the farm? ______________________________
5. What can the pupils do? ______________________________
6. What can they visit later? ______________________________
7. What can they have? ______________________________

(9) **Complete the sentences and think of suitable words.**

grandma's little farm

Grandma has a little farm.

In her living room there is a ____________________ in the aquarium.

In her garden she has ____________________. Grandma gives them carrots.

The ____________________ barks.

The ____________________ lies on the bed.

The ____________________ says the same things we say.

The ____________________ are on the fields and eat grass.

⑩ Animals are great, because they give us many things which we use. Think of suitable words.

 →  1. *Cows give milk.*

 → 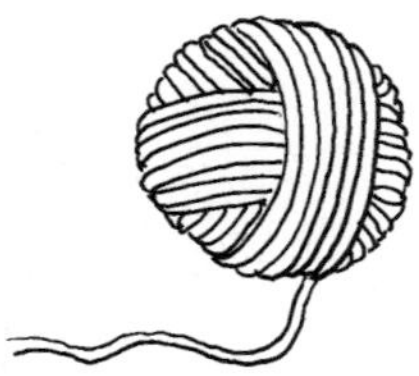 2. ______________________________

 →  3. ______________________________

 →  4. ______________________________

 →  5. ______________________________

⑪ Have you got a pet? Answer the questions.

1. Have you got a pet? ______________________________
2. Have you got a dog? ______________________________
3. Has your neighbour got a cat? ______________________________
4. Has your teacher got a fish? ______________________________
4. Has your grandfather got a farm? ______________________________
5. Has your sister got a guinea pig? ______________________________
6. Has your best friend got a tortoise? ______________________________

6 days and months - Übersichtsseite

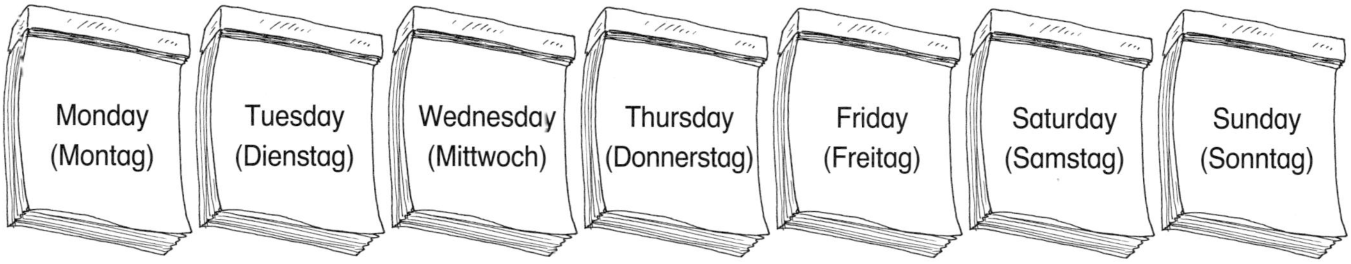

January (Januar)

February (Februar)

March (März)

April (April)

May (Mai)

June (Juni)

July (Juli)

August (August)

September (September)

October (Oktober)

November (November)

December (Dezember)

6 days and months 1

1 Find the days of the week.
Finde die Wochentage.

K	K	F	F	R	I	D	A	Y	F	A	U
Y	Z	H	L	L	F	J	M	Q	C	R	W
W	X	H	K	F	P	S	U	N	D	A	Y
I	M	F	A	Y	U	T	P	X	F	G	F
S	Q	T	H	U	R	S	D	A	Y	K	T
Q	F	Y	K	Q	U	A	B	J	R	H	U
P	W	E	D	N	E	S	D	A	Y	K	E
A	S	Q	B	W	S	D	U	L	R	E	S
L	S	A	T	U	R	D	A	Y	X	H	D
L	Y	M	V	G	N	O	Z	G	C	A	A
G	R	M	L	R	X	F	S	Q	R	L	Y
Q	F	M	O	N	D	A	Y	S	V	U	K

6 days and months 2

2 Find the months of the year.
Finde die Monate eines Jahres.

B	Q	P	V	F	N	L	F	O	C	T	O	B	E	R
D	W	Q	X	X	I	S	M	D	P	M	W	Q	U	K
F	K	U	V	M	R	E	H	A	P	R	I	L	U	J
A	M	A	R	C	H	J	D	U	H	T	S	X	N	D
K	E	P	V	T	T	V	N	O	V	E	M	B	E	R
U	H	P	R	U	V	D	R	C	Q	E	O	S	G	C
F	Q	F	B	S	X	J	F	E	B	R	U	A	R	Y
B	B	W	T	J	Y	A	B	V	V	S	F	Q	F	K
A	A	M	A	Y	P	D	E	J	A	N	U	A	R	Y
U	G	U	C	V	B	H	Q	H	Y	K	Z	X	F	V
G	E	J	E	H	I	G	D	E	C	E	M	B	E	R
U	T	U	E	E	M	U	J	Y	L	N	U	R	T	C
S	S	L	J	S	E	P	T	E	M	B	E	R	D	Y
T	G	Y	H	F	D	Q	E	T	F	T	B	B	I	V
S	C	X	F	F	O	J	U	N	E	L	U	O	E	F

6 days and months 3

3 Find the days and months.
Finde die Tage und Monate.

1. It is the first day of the week.
2. It is the last school day of the week.
3. What is the last month of the year?
4. What is the third month of the year?
5. In this month it is very hot and sunny.
6. The day after Tuesday is …
7. The month after April is …
8. In this month it rains a lot.
9. There is no school on …
10. The first day of the weekend is …
11. What is the month before December?
12. It is the fourth month of the year.
13. What is the month after August?
14. Sometimes summer holidays start in …
15. What is the sixth month of the year?

4 Write down the days of the week.
Schreibe die Wochentage auf.

6 days and months 4

5 What month is it?
Kennst du den Monat?

J ______________________________

F ______________________________

M ______________________________

A ______________________________

M ______________________________

J ______________________________

J ______________________________

A ______________________________

S ______________________________

O ______________________________

N ______________________________

D ______________________________

6 dates

1 What date is it? Match the English and the German date.
Verbinde das englische und das deutsche Datum.

			Number
①	**8. Januar 1998**	21st July 1980	*11*
②	**3. Mai 2015**	31st May 2019	*15*
③	**1. Dezember 2016**	18th February 2003	
④	**24. September 2020**	2nd October 1999	
⑤	**22. August 2017**	1st December 2016	
⑥	**2. Oktober 1999**	28th December 2020	
⑦	**12. März 2002**	23rd November 2015	
⑧	**23. November 2015**	30th January 2011	
⑨	**18. Februar 2003**	24th September 2020	
⑩	**20. Juni 1993**	26th April 2009	
⑪	**21. Juli 1980**	20th June 1993	
⑫	**26. April 2009**	22nd August 2017	
⑬	**28. Dezember 2020**	12th March 2002	
⑭	**30. Januar 2011**	3rd May 2015	
⑮	**31. Mai 2019**	8th January 1998	

6 days and months 1

1 **Find the days of the week.**

Q	Q	Q	B	U	K	L	K	W	M	F	S	N	S
D	Z	T	P	W	Q	M	T	M	O	N	D	A	Y
F	S	A	T	U	R	D	A	Y	Q	Z	J	L	N
G	E	H	H	G	P	G	W	G	Y	S	T	S	L
D	E	B	H	F	W	U	A	H	Y	I	U	H	Y
F	F	R	I	D	A	Y	X	B	W	O	E	X	C
K	T	Q	D	X	Y	J	S	G	E	V	S	L	M
V	H	Z	O	G	S	X	U	F	D	L	D	D	R
F	U	I	Y	C	M	D	N	Q	N	B	A	D	H
Q	R	U	N	S	F	U	D	K	E	W	Y	H	N
Q	S	B	V	L	R	F	A	T	S	C	L	I	Z
B	D	P	D	Q	F	E	Y	N	D	N	R	W	Y
N	A	C	C	R	Q	B	C	C	A	J	C	T	B
B	Y	H	L	J	W	X	M	I	Y	D	C	S	Q

6 days and months 2

② **Find the months of the year.**

F	H	M	F	D	T	N	T	W	P	X	V	O	L	H	B	U	Q
K	P	R	S	W	V	O	C	S	S	R	R	I	S	D	S	V	E
N	H	V	O	H	U	V	C	J	H	L	C	I	P	D	B	F	J
T	R	E	Q	M	D	E	N	N	Q	H	S	B	F	R	X	F	A
F	E	W	V	A	N	M	F	O	T	U	C	S	A	F	F	O	N
Z	G	H	S	R	O	B	J	H	M	Z	V	E	P	U	E	W	U
G	N	C	S	C	O	E	L	S	Z	R	N	P	R	I	B	X	A
M	L	X	R	H	X	R	C	K	M	X	X	T	I	Z	R	X	R
E	C	N	G	C	T	S	L	J	L	Q	B	E	L	J	U	K	Y
G	W	K	S	F	D	K	Q	U	J	E	S	M	V	V	A	W	U
B	R	U	V	L	U	S	O	L	I	O	A	B	T	P	R	J	S
S	L	C	E	L	U	W	G	Y	Q	J	U	E	Q	G	Y	H	Z
N	R	I	D	E	C	E	M	B	E	R	G	R	E	L	Y	D	H
T	J	F	N	O	L	B	M	H	R	C	U	L	R	U	R	H	I
C	H	R	M	P	P	W	A	S	P	V	S	K	G	V	O	I	T
P	M	D	Y	K	T	L	Y	U	B	O	T	D	M	G	E	G	F
P	O	Q	X	Q	Q	V	P	A	O	C	T	O	B	E	R	S	C
M	J	U	N	E	J	K	K	H	I	R	K	J	M	X	Z	G	W

6 days and months 3

③ **Find the days and months.**

1. It is the first day of the week.
2. It is the last school day in the week.
3. What is the last month of the year?
4. What is the third month of the year?
5. In this month it is very hot and sunny.
6. The day after Tuesday is …
7. The month after April is …
8. In this month it rains a lot.
9. There is no school on …
10. The first day of the weekend is …
11. What is the month before December?
12. It is the fourth month of the year.
13. What is the month after August?
14. Sometimes summer holidays start in …
15. What is the sixth month of the year?

④ **Write down the days of the week.**

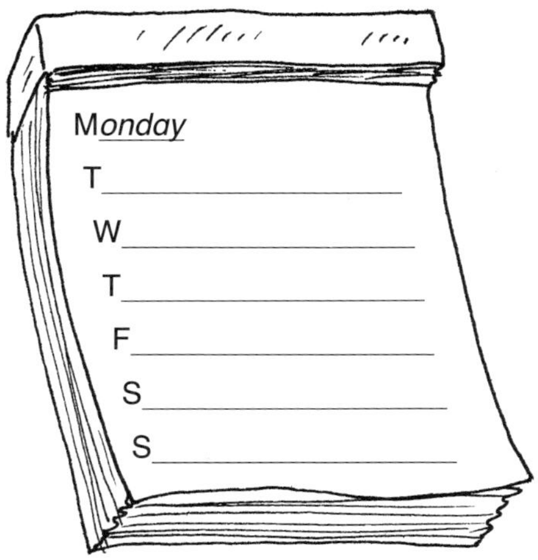

⑤ **What month is it?**

6 dates

① **What date is it? Write the English and the German date.**

8.1.1998	8th January 1998	8. Januar 1998
3.5.2015	______________	______________
1.12.2016	______________	______________
24.9.2020	______________	______________
22.8.2017	______________	______________
2.10.1999	______________	______________
12.3.2002	______________	______________
23.11.2015	______________	______________
18.2.2003	______________	______________
20.6.1993	______________	______________
21.7.1980	______________	______________
26.4.2009	______________	______________
28.12.2020	______________	______________
30.1.2011	______________	______________
31.5.2019	______________	______________

times - Übersichtsseite

Uhrzeiten:

ten to eight

07:50

seven fifty

quarter past nine

09:15

nine fifteen

half past ten

10:30

ten thirty

quarter to eleven

10:45

ten forty-five

twelve o'clock / midday / midnight

12:00

twelve o'clock

one o'clock

01:00

one o'clock

eight o'clock

08:00

eight o'clock

twenty to three

02:40

two forty

7 times 1

1 What time is it? Match the time with the words.
Verbinde die Uhrzeit mit den Wörtern.

It's quarter past 6.

It's 25 past 2.

It's half past 3.

It's quarter to 10.

It's 10 to 2.

02:30

07:40

06:37

03:05

01:25

It's 5 past 3.

It's 6 thirty-seven.

It's half past 2.

It's 1 twenty-five.

It's 20 to 8.

2 What time is it? Draw the time.
Wie spät ist es? Zeichne die Uhrzeit.

It's quarter to 3.

It's half past 9.

It's 5 o'clock.

It's 6 twenty-three.

It's 9 forty-two.

It's 10 past ten.

3 Oscar's day

Write sentences about Oscar's day. What time is it? Use the ideas in the box.
Schreibe über Oscars Tag. Wie spät ist es? Verwende die Ideen in der Box.

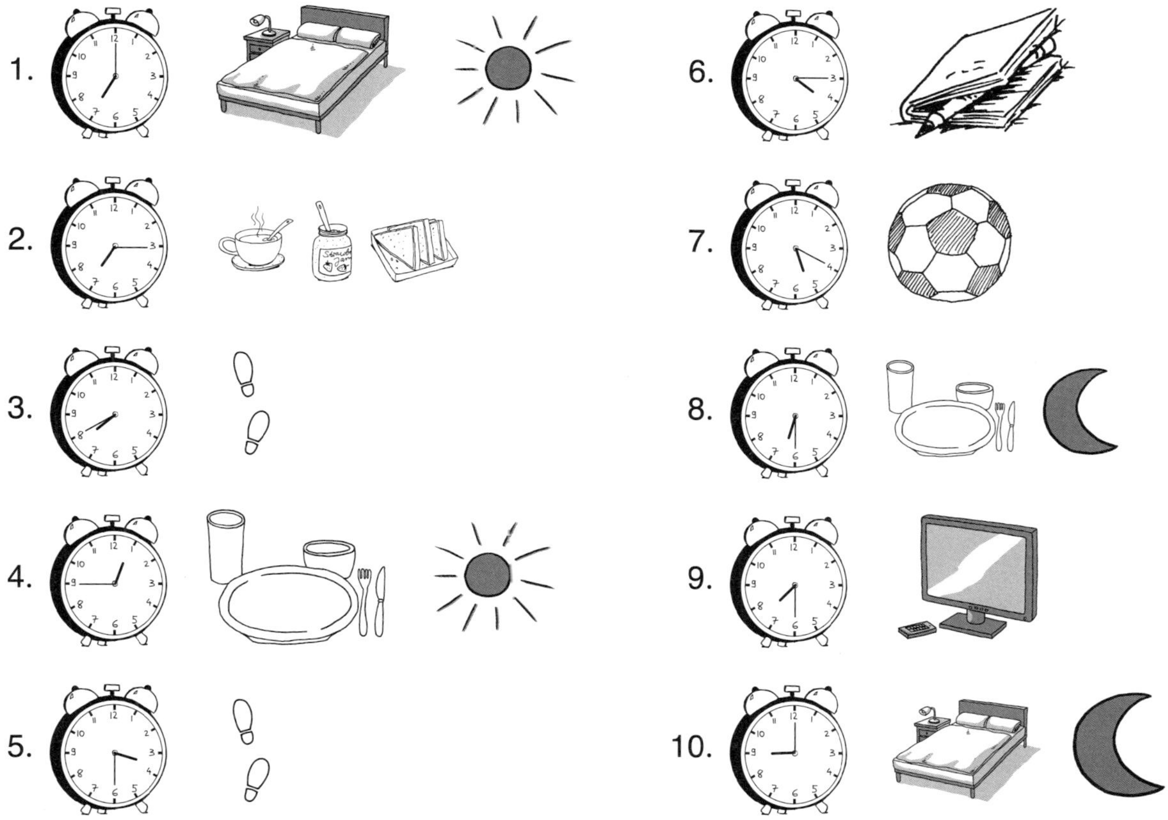

~~has breakfast~~ – does homework – has dinner – has lunch – goes to bed – ~~gets up~~ – goes to school – comes back from school – watches TV – plays football

1. Oscar **gets up** at seven o'clock.

2. Oscar **has breakfast** at quarter past seven.

3. ______________________________ at twenty to eight.

4. ______________________________ at quarter to one.

5. ______________________________ at half past three.

6. ______________________________ at quarter past four.

7. ______________________________ at twenty past five.

8. ______________________________ at half past six.

9. ______________________________ at half past seven.

10. ______________________________ at nine o'clock.

7 times 1

① **What time is it? Write the time.**

 *It's quarter past six.*

06:37 *It's six thirty-seven.*

09:40

01:25

14:30

15:05

17:16

12:00

② **What time is it? Draw the time.**

 It's quarter to three.

It's six twenty-three.

 It's quarter past twelve.

It's four thirty-eight.

 It's half past nine.

It's eleven oh two.

 It's five o'clock.

It's nine forty-two.

3 Oscar's day

Write sentences about Oscar's day. What time is it? Use the ideas in the box.

1. 

2. 

3. 

4. 

5. 

6. 

7. 

8. 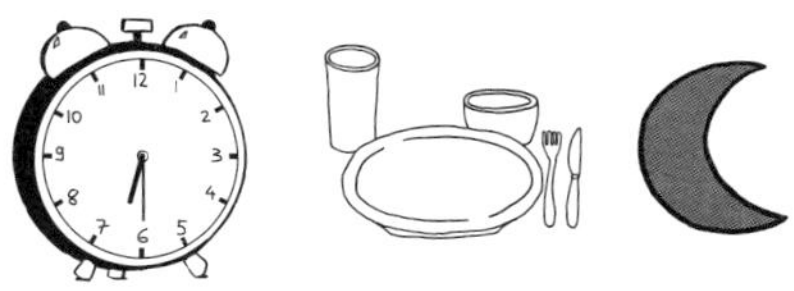

9. 

10. 

go to bed – ~~get up~~ – go to school – have lunch – watch TV – come back from school – play football – ~~have breakfast~~ – have dinner – do homework

1. Oscar **gets up** at seven o'clock.
2. Oscar **has breakfast** at quarter past seven.
3. ______________________________
4. ______________________________
5. ______________________________
6. ______________________________
7. ______________________________.
8. ______________________________
9. ______________________________
10. ______________________________

8 numbers and colours - Übersichtsseite

1 → one | 2 → two | 3 → three | 4 → four | 5 → five | 6 → six | 7 → seven | 8 → eight | 9 → nine | 10 → ten | 11 → eleven | 12 → twelve | 13 → thirteen | 14 → fourteen | 15 → fifteen | 16 → sixteen | 17 → seventeen | 18 → eighteen | 19 → nineteen | 20 → twenty | 21 → twenty-one | 22 → twenty-two | 24 → twenty-four | 30 → thirty | 35 → thirty-five | 36 → thirty-six | 40 → forty | 47 → forty-seven | 50 → fifty | 58 → fifty-eight | 60 → sixty | 69 → sixty-nine | 70 → seventy | 80 → eighty | 90 → ninety | 100 → one hundred

1st	first
2nd	second
3rd	third
4th	fourth
5th	fifth
6th	sixth
7th	seventh
8th	eighth
9th	ninth
10th	tenth
11th	eleventh
12th	twelfth
13th	thirteenth
14th	fourteenth
15th	fifteenth
16th	sixteenth
17th	seventeenth
18th	eighteenth
19th	nineteenth
20th	twentieth
21st	twenty-first
22nd	twenty-second
23rd	twenty-third
24th	twenty-fourth
25th	twenty-fifth
30th	thirtieth
40th	fortieth
50th	fiftieth
60th	sixtieth
70th	seventieth
80th	eightieth
90th	ninetieth

blue → blau
red → rot
green → grün
pink → pink
brown → braun
orange → orange
grey → grau
purple → lila
black → schwarz
yellow → gelb

8 numbers 1

1 Write the number next to the word.
Schreibe die Zahl neben das Wort.

77	101	3	10	6	55	9	11	60	100
40	~~99~~	1	70	22	4	30	7	66	10
90	33	2	20	88	5	44	8	50	~~80~~

eighty _80_ seventy-seven ____ one ____ ten ____ two ____ twenty-two ____

three ____ five ____ eighty-eight ____ four ____ eleven ____ six ____ seven ____

eight ____ ninety ____ nine ____ twenty ____ forty ____ thirty ____

sixty ____ fifty ____ seventy ____ one hundred ____ thirty-three ____ forty-four ____

ten ____ fifty-five ____ sixty-six ____ ninety-nine _99_ one hundred and one ____

2 Can you find the numbers?
Findest du die Zahlen?

B	B	Q	T	E	N	T	H	W	T	H	I	R	D
E	B	P	M	T	Q	D	S	H	K	N	D	O	G
S	T	W	E	N	T	I	E	T	H	O	L	F	S
U	R	L	P	G	L	M	W	C	Q	P	W	G	T
F	I	R	S	T	L	O	W	P	C	M	F	R	L
P	J	N	A	C	Z	T	W	E	L	F	T	H	R
N	L	A	C	O	S	B	M	P	R	B	Q	G	M
I	E	T	H	I	R	T	I	E	T	H	A	Y	E
N	R	C	H	H	C	R	Q	H	N	E	O	G	K
T	Q	F	I	Z	W	O	K	S	N	L	L	H	P
H	H	Y	Y	N	S	E	V	E	N	T	H	E	H
M	X	D	W	B	P	L	V	S	C	G	G	G	V
B	K	L	V	V	K	C	B	U	F	I	F	T	H
Z	S	E	C	O	N	D	Q	E	A	S	Q	L	L

first
second
third
fifth
seventh
ninth
tenth
twelfth
twentieth
thirtieth

3 Write the numbers.
Schreibe die Zahlen.

1 one	1st first
2 ____________	2nd ____________
3 ____________	3rd ____________
4 ____________	4th ____________
5 ____________	5th ____________

five, two, four, three –
fifth, second, fourth, third

8 numbers 2

4 Find the numbers.
Finde die Zahlen.

X	E	F	O	R	T	Y	-	F	I	V	E	U	V	W	U	M	N	I	R
I	X	V	E	J	U	D	S	N	T	T	G	Y	N	D	L	Q	I	Z	J
M	N	I	N	E	T	Y	-	S	E	V	E	N	I	R	F	T	I	X	Z
J	U	P	T	B	N	I	C	J	J	O	D	C	K	X	Q	F	M	Y	C
T	X	Y	E	O	G	Q	B	Y	O	S	J	L	S	L	B	M	T	H	S
W	U	T	U	Z	O	N	I	N	E	T	Y	-	S	I	X	R	W	H	I
E	S	N	J	H	U	R	V	V	O	Y	D	N	J	Q	M	Y	E	R	X
L	S	O	S	F	I	F	T	Y	-	N	I	N	E	H	X	W	N	Q	T
V	W	G	N	W	K	H	Z	X	L	D	L	T	L	E	N	C	T	U	Y
E	B	E	S	E	V	E	N	T	Y	-	O	N	E	O	I	D	Y	Y	-
D	N	F	C	J	M	G	Q	W	E	Y	K	D	U	B	N	M	-	Q	T
O	B	K	T	C	M	A	F	E	C	L	X	P	H	W	E	N	T	S	W
T	H	I	R	T	Y	-	F	O	U	R	X	Z	K	O	T	R	H	Y	O
B	N	H	C	S	Q	W	T	G	Q	U	T	M	J	R	E	R	R	P	H
J	S	I	X	T	Y	-	E	I	G	H	T	V	T	O	E	J	E	H	K
Q	I	B	Q	U	N	Q	G	K	J	F	A	H	H	C	N	F	E	R	R
T	X	W	D	F	T	Q	I	J	S	A	C	Y	S	J	K	X	N	I	D
Q	F	B	G	B	L	E	I	G	H	T	Y	-	E	I	G	H	T	K	R
O	Y	Q	F	F	F	I	U	T	I	L	M	H	O	W	Q	R	B	G	P
Y	F	I	F	T	E	E	N	G	T	H	I	R	T	Y	-	N	I	N	E

twelve
thirty-four
seventy-one
sixty-eight
eighty-eight
forty-five
~~twenty-three~~
thirty-nine
ninety-seven
fifty-nine
sixty-two
ninety-six
nineteen
fifteen

5 What number is it? Write the letters in the gaps.
Schreibe die Buchstaben in die Lücken.

25 twenty-__ __ __ __
13 thir__ __ __ __
12 tw__ __ __ __
19 nine__ __ __ __
20 tw__ __ __ __
69 sixty-__ __ __ __
79 seventy-__ __ __ __
80 ei__ __ __ __
99 ninety-__ __ __ __
83 eighty-__ __ __ __ __
68 sixty-__ __ __ __ __

29 twenty-__ __ __ __
37 thirty-__ __ __ __ __
36 thirty-__ __ __
40 fo__ __ __
43 forty-__ __ __ __ __
90 ni__ __ __ __
70 se__ __ __ __ __
82 eighty-__ __ __
95 ninety-__ __ __ __
74 seventy-__ __ __ __

49 forty-__ __ __ __
50 fi__ __ __
51 fifty-__ __ __
60 si__ __ __
67 sixty-__ __ __ __ __

8 numbers 1

① **Write the numbers.**

1	3	4	5	7	8
______	______	______	______	______	______
9	10	20	40	50	60
______	______	______	______	______	______
80	100	11	44	55	77
______	______	______	______	______	______

② **Can you find the numbers?**

H	E	P	Q	Q	N	H	S	H	U	Q	U	U	L	A	Y
T	P	U	F	H	L	N	E	S	T	N	T	S	V	J	U
V	V	Y	Q	I	K	I	C	R	O	V	X	W	C	P	V
Y	T	R	B	S	L	B	O	Z	J	P	V	Z	O	E	T
U	I	C	M	I	G	O	N	J	N	R	I	T	Z	L	E
E	T	Q	H	F	S	J	D	I	X	F	L	C	I	D	N
C	M	I	T	O	V	N	C	L	J	K	R	W	B	Q	T
C	Q	F	H	Q	V	N	T	W	E	N	T	I	E	T	H
A	G	I	I	G	X	I	M	P	C	E	N	T	F	U	H
Q	M	R	R	N	N	N	V	K	U	R	J	W	N	U	A
T	V	S	T	M	H	T	C	J	Q	T	R	E	T	X	F
K	W	T	I	H	L	H	L	M	U	S	W	L	H	R	I
R	Y	W	E	K	T	P	K	P	Y	M	J	F	I	G	F
P	S	J	T	S	E	V	E	N	T	H	S	T	R	L	T
H	I	U	H	K	F	C	G	N	V	Q	G	H	D	S	H
N	K	I	E	T	B	W	N	Q	X	T	L	D	M	X	T

first
second
third
fifth
seventh
nineth
tenth
twelfth
twentieth
thirtieth

③ **Write the numbers.**

1 one	1st first
2 ______	2nd ______
3 ______	3rd ______
4 ______	4th ______
5 ______	5th ______

8 numbers 2

④ Find the numbers.

K	V	G	X	I	O	S	Z	N	K	M	Y	E	N	O	R	W	D	B	E	U	K	G
Y	U	J	O	B	P	P	W	M	Z	Y	S	T	H	I	R	T	Y	-	F	O	U	R
S	Y	N	L	T	O	L	W	B	A	A	Y	L	V	D	X	J	J	T	F	H	W	W
H	X	L	X	F	I	F	T	Y	-	N	I	N	E	K	D	W	H	L	S	E	S	T
N	G	J	E	U	Y	X	S	X	R	J	E	R	J	S	W	W	Y	D	E	F	E	X
A	Y	U	G	T	J	Q	K	E	P	G	D	F	A	T	R	F	Q	H	V	Z	J	X
Q	D	U	Z	W	C	Y	T	H	I	R	T	Y	-	N	I	N	E	I	E	J	O	T
V	S	V	T	C	E	K	X	W	F	P	N	Q	J	B	J	K	U	L	N	C	M	Q
Z	S	E	W	O	O	E	E	Z	C	R	R	E	P	Y	T	L	U	Q	T	F	Z	F
X	C	M	E	C	G	F	E	I	G	H	T	Y	-	E	I	G	H	T	Y	I	P	T
T	P	N	L	R	Y	Z	Y	B	Y	M	Y	B	W	F	B	C	C	I	-	F	U	C
G	X	X	V	R	P	N	S	I	X	T	Y	-	E	I	G	H	T	T	O	T	T	V
N	W	P	E	V	N	F	D	S	F	G	E	P	L	T	C	N	R	U	N	E	G	U
F	B	L	V	F	D	T	X	O	O	P	X	Y	J	U	Q	D	X	N	E	E	H	N
F	D	V	R	O	N	I	N	E	T	Y	-	S	I	X	S	U	F	P	Q	N	S	I
R	E	R	E	R	X	E	F	S	V	G	F	L	V	D	S	B	M	L	T	N	J	N
C	E	A	Z	T	I	X	S	N	T	W	E	N	T	Y	-	T	H	R	E	E	S	E
W	A	Y	X	Y	S	I	X	T	Y	-	T	W	O	C	K	U	S	I	T	Y	M	T
L	O	Y	O	-	V	S	Z	R	I	S	J	O	I	R	H	N	U	W	K	P	K	E
N	O	D	I	F	F	W	Z	A	B	Q	O	R	O	I	H	D	R	X	K	M	R	E
G	A	V	R	I	S	S	Q	T	J	K	L	G	P	S	K	A	J	X	H	C	O	N
U	J	X	M	V	W	M	K	Q	M	N	I	N	E	T	Y	-	S	E	V	E	N	V
D	O	U	T	E	J	S	K	B	B	R	P	G	A	Y	U	S	I	E	T	Z	E	J

twelve
thirty-four
seventy-one
sixty-eight
eighty-eight
forty-five
~~twenty-three~~
thirty-nine
ninety-seven
fifty-nine
sixty-two
ninety-six
nineteen
fifteen

⑤ What number is it? Write the letters in the gaps.

25 t _ _ _ _ _ _ _ _ _ _

13 t _ _ _ _ _ _ _

12 t _ _ _ _ _

19 n _ _ _ _ _ _ _

20 t _ _ _ _ _

29 t _ _ _ _ _ _ _ _ _ _

37 t _ _ _ _ _ _ _ _ _ _ _

36 t _ _ _ _ _ _ _ _ _

40 f _ _ _ _

43 f _ _ _ _ _ _ _ _ _ _

49 f _ _ _ _ _ _ _ _ _

50 f _ _ _ _

74 s _ _ _ _ _ _ _ _ _ _ _

51 f _ _ _ _ _ _ _ _

60 s _ _ _ _

67 s _ _ _ _ _ _ _ _ _ _

69 s _ _ _ _ _ _ _ _ _

70 s _ _ _ _ _ _

79 s _ _ _ _ _ _ _ _ _ _ _

80 e _ _ _ _ _

82 e _ _ _ _ _ _ _ _ _

90 n _ _ _ _ _

99 n _ _ _ _ _ _ _ _ _ _

95 n _ _ _ _ _ _ _ _ _ _

83 e _ _ _ _ _ _ _ _ _ _ _

68 s _ _ _ _ _ _ _ _ _ _

8 colours 1

1 What colours do you know? Colour the school things and complete the sentences.
Male die Schulsachen an und vervollständige die Sätze.

1.  The rubber is ____________________________________.
2.  The school bag is ________________________________.
3.  The pencil is ____________________________________.
4.  The exercise book is _____________________________.
5.  The pencil case is _______________________________.
6. 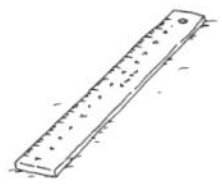 The ruler is _____________________________________.

2 Answer the questions.
Beantworte die Fragen.

1.  What's your favourite colour? ______________________
2.  What colour is your pencil case? ___________________
3.  What colour is your rubber? _______________________
4.  What colour is your school bag? ___________________
5. 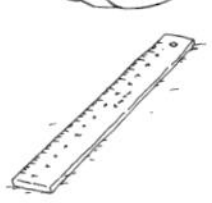 What colour is your ruler? _______________________
6.  What colour is your pen? _________________________

3 Colour the bears.
Male die Bären aus.

4 Colour David and his bike.
Male David und sein Fahrrad an.

1. David's cap is yellow.
2. David's T-shirt is red.
3. David's jeans are blue.
4. David's bike is green.
5. David's shoes are brown.
6. David's socks are black and white.
7. David's school bag is black.

5 Read about Henry's favourite colours and answer the questions.
Lies den Text und setze ein Häkchen hinter die richtige Antwort.

Henry loves all colours. His favourite colour is blue. His room has blue walls. His bed is green and his desk is red. His chair is yellow. Henry's school bag is brown. There are coloured pencils in his blue pencil case. He has a blue, a green, a brown, a yellow and a purple felt tip. When he plays football with his friends he wears his blue shirt and his white shorts. His football is white and black and his football shoes are white and black, too.

1. What is Henry's favourite colour? ☐ blue ☐ green
2. What colour has the bed? ☐ green ☐ red
3. What is the colour of his chair? ☐ yellow ☐ blue
4. What colour is his pencil case? ☐ purple ☐ blue
5. What colour has his football? ☐ white / black ☐ white / blue

8 colours 1

1 **What colours do you know? Colour the school things and write sentences.**

1. The rubber is blue.
2. The school bag is ______________________________

3. The ____________________________________
4. ______________________________________

5. ______________________________________
6. ______________________________________

7. ______________________________________
8. ______________________________________

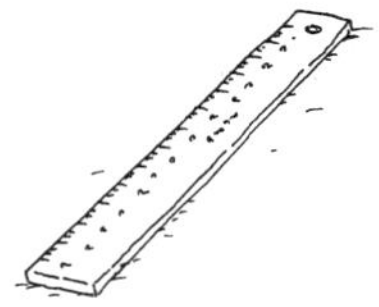

9. ______________________________________

2 **Answer the questions.**

1. What's your favourite colour? My favourite colour is ______________________
2. What colour is your pencil case? ______________________________
3. What colour is your rubber? ______________________________
4. What colour is your school bag? ______________________________
5. What colour is your ruler? ______________________________
6. What colour is your pen? ______________________________
7. What colour is your pencil? ______________________________

3 **Colour the bears and write down the colour.**

__________ __________ __________ __________ __________ __________ __________

8 colours 2

④ **Colour David and his bike.**

1. David's cap is yellow.
2. David's T-shirt is red.
3. David's jeans are blue.
4. David's bike is green.
5. David's shoes are brown.
6. David's socks are black and white.
7. David's school bag is black.

⑤ **What are Henry's favourite colours?**
Read about Henry's favourite colours and answer the questions.

Henry loves all colours. His favourite colour is blue. His room has blue walls. His bed is green and his desk is red. His chair is yellow. Henry's school bag is brown. There are coloured pencils in his blue pencil case. He has a blue, a green, a brown, a yellow and a purple felt tip. When he plays football with his friends he wears his blue shirt and his white shorts. His football is white and black and his football shoes are white and black, too.

1. What is Henry's favourite colour? ______________________
2. What colour has the bed? ______________________
3. Is his chair brown? ______________________
4. What colour is his pencil case? ______________________
5. What does Henry wear when he plays football? ______________________
6. What colour has his football? ______________________
7. Are his shoes white and green? ______________________

9

my party – Übersichtsseite

happy birthday
(Herzlichen Glückwunsch)

birthday (Geburtstag)

invitation card
(Einladungskarte)

birthday party / sleepover party
(Geburtstagsparty / Übernachtungsparty),
celebrate (feiern), have a birthday party
(eine Geburtstagsparty geben)

cake (Kuchen), chocolate cake
(Schokoladenkuchen)

drinks (Getränke)

present (Geschenk)

candle (Kerze)

biscuits (Kekse)

decorate (dekorieren)

guests (Gäste)

birthday list
(Geburtstagsliste)

music (Musik)

9 my party 1

1 Look at Jake's party food. Are they right or wrong? Tick your answer.
Schau dir Jakes Partyessen an und lies die Sätze. Richtig oder falsch? Kreuze an.

	right	wrong
1. Jake has chicken at his party.	☐	☐
2. Jake has vegetables at his party.	☐	☐
3. His party food is cake and orange juice.	☐	☐
4. I can see biscuits.	☐	☐
5. I can see cola.	☐	☐
6. They drink tea and coffee.	☐	☐
7. They eat sausages.	☐	☐
8. Jake has a bag of crisps.	☐	☐
9. I can see a plate of chips.	☐	☐
10. His party food is toast and cheese.	☐	☐
11. They eat chocolate at the party.	☐	☐

2 Sarah invites a lot of friends to her birthday party. Complete the words.
Sarah lädt viele Freunde zu ihrer Party ein. Vervollständige die Wörter.

shopping for my party

– biscuits	– toa________
– co________	– cri________
– orange________	– cak________
– chick________	– choc________
– chee________	– saus________

my party 2

3 Look at the invitation card for the sleepover party and tick the right answer.
Schau dir die Einladung an und setze ein Häkchen hinter die richtige Antwort.

Dear friends,

I want to celebrate my birthday with you.

Please come to my sleepover party!

Where: at my flat

When: May 7th, at 4 o'clock

Where I live: at 5 Kingston Road

What you need: pyjamas, brush

What we do: It's a surprise.

Love, Sam

1. Who is the invitation from?	from Ben ☐	from Sam ☐
2. When is the birthday party?	May 7th ☐	April 11th ☐
3. What time is the birthday party?	3 o'clock ☐	4 o'clock ☐
4. What do the guests need?	money ☐	pyjamas ☐

4 Birthday party
Read the texts and find the differences. Underline them.
Lies die Texte und finde die Unterschiede zwischen Text A und B. Unterstreiche sie.

A: It's a big birthday party and all friends are here. They are dancing and laughing. My favourite cake is on the table. I love chocolate cake. There are bottles of water and lemonade on the table. My parents are in the garden, my dog is on the sofa. My best friend takes pictures of all guests. There are many presents on the table. My sister is singing and dancing. Some friends are playing football in the garden. We have lots of fun together.

B: It's a big birthday party and all friends are here. They are dancing and laughing. My favourite biscuits are on the table. I love chocolate biscuits. There are sandwiches and sausages on the table. My parents are in the living room, my dog is on the chair. My best friend takes pictures of all guests. There are many presents on the table. My brother is singing and dancing. Some friends are playing basketball in the garden. We have lots of fun together.

5 Liz prepares her party. Find the information in the text and circle them yellow.
Suche die Informationen der Einladung im Text und kreise diese gelb ein.

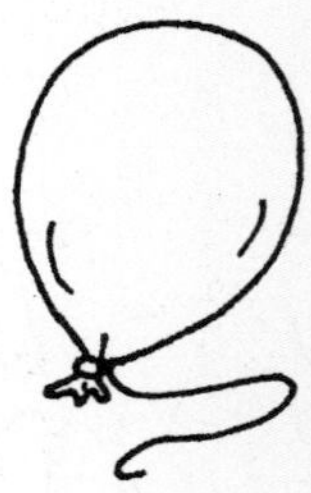

Liz' birthday party

When: next week, March 16th
Where we meet: swimming hall
What time: 2 o'clock
Food: sausages, buiscuits, chocolate cake
What we do: go swimming, celebrate at home
What you need: swimsuit, pyjamas, brush

Love, Liz

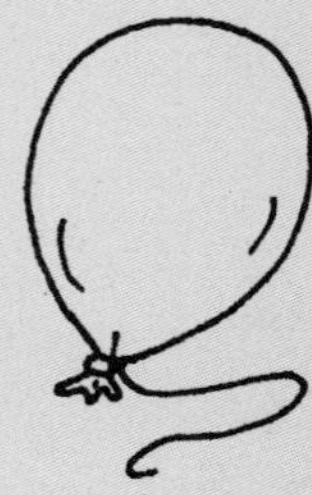

My birthday is next week. So I need to write a list about all things I need and write the invitation cards. The party will be on March 16th. I want to go swimming with my friends. When we are back at home, we can eat sandwiches. Mum must buy all the things that I need. I want to have lemonade and sausages. I hope she prepares a chocolate cake and buys buiscuits. My friends can stay at my house and sleep here. But they need pyjamas and brushes. We meet at 2 o'clock at the swimming hall. I hope they can come and don't forget their swimsuits.

6 Match the questions with the answers.
Verbinde die Fragen mit den Antworten.

1. Why does Liz write invitation cards?	Because Liz wants to go swimming.
2. Why do they need pyjamas and brushes?	Because Liz wants to eat sandwiches and sausages.
3. Why don't they go to the park?	Because Liz has a sleepover party.
4. Why does Liz's mother go shopping?	Because she loves chocolate.
5. Why does Liz want a chocolate cake?	Because it's her birthday next week.

7 When is your party and what do you want to do? Write the words down.
Wann ist deine Gebrtstagsparty? Schreibe auf, was du machen möchtest. Was musst du dafür einkaufen? Ergänze die Begriffe.

Nadja Brize, Amel Selmi: Wortschatz 5. Klasse – Inklusionsmaterial

9 my party 1

(1) **Look at Jake's party food. Write sentences.**

1. Jake wants to have sausages at his party.
2. I can see ______________________________
3. His party food is ______________________________
4. ______________________________
5. ______________________________
6. ______________________________
7. ______________________________
8. ______________________________

(2) **Sarah invites a lot of friends to her birthday party. Write down 10 things she maybe wants to buy.**

shopping for my party

– biscuits	– ____________
– ____________	– ____________
– ____________	– ____________
– ____________	– ____________
– ____________	– ____________
– ____________	– ____________

9 my party 2

③ **Answer the questions.**

Dear friends,

I want to celebrate my birthday with you.
Please come to my sleepover party!
Where: at my flat
When: May 7th, at 4 o'clock
Where I live: at 5 Kingston Road
What you need: pyjamas, brush
What we do: It's a surprise.

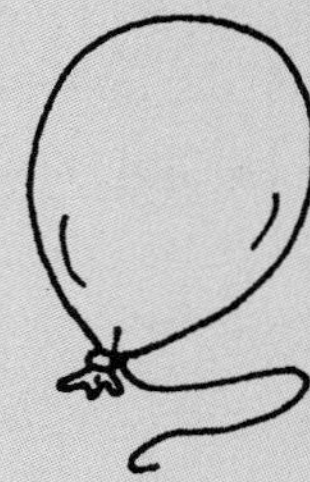

Love, Sam

1. Who is the invitation from? ____________________
2. When is the birthday party? ____________________
3. What time is the birthday party? ____________________
4. What do the guests need? ____________________

④ **Birthday party**

Read the texts and find the differences. Underline them.

A: It's a big birthday party and all friends are here. They are dancing and laughing. My favourite cake is in the kitchen. I love chocolate cake. There are bottles of water and lemonade on the table. My parents are in the living room, my dog is on the sofa. My best friend takes pictures of all guests. There are many presents on the table. My sister is eating and drinking. Some friends are playing basketball in the garden. We have lots of fun together.

B: It's a big birthday party and all friends are here. They are dancing and laughing. My favourite cake is in the kitchen. I love chocolate cake. There are sandwiches and sausages on the table. My parents are in the living room, my dog is on the sofa. My best friend takes pictures of all guests. There are many presents on the table. My sister is eating and drinking. Some friends are playing basketball in the garden. We have lots of fun together.

C: It's a big birthday party and all friends are here. They are swimming in the pool. My favourite biscuits are on the table. I love chocolate biscuits. My parents are in the garden, my dog is on the chair. My best friend takes pictures of all guests. There are many presents on the floor. My sister is singing and talking. Some friends are playing football in the house. We have lots of fun together.

my party 3

⑤ **Liz prepares her party. Read the text and complete the invitation card.**

Liz's birthday party

My birthday is next week. So I need to write a list about all things I need and write the invitation cards. The party will be on March 16th. I want to go swimming with my friends. When we are back at home, we can eat sandwiches. Mum must buy all the things that I need. I want to have lemonade and sausages. I hope she prepares a chocolate cake and buys buiscuits. My friends can stay at my house and sleep here. But they need pyjamas and brushes. We meet at 2 o'clock at the swimming hall. I hope they can come and don't forget their swimsuits.

invitation to my party

When: ______________________________

Where we meet: ______________________________

What time: ______________________________

Food: ______________________________

What we do: ______________________________

What you need: ______________________________

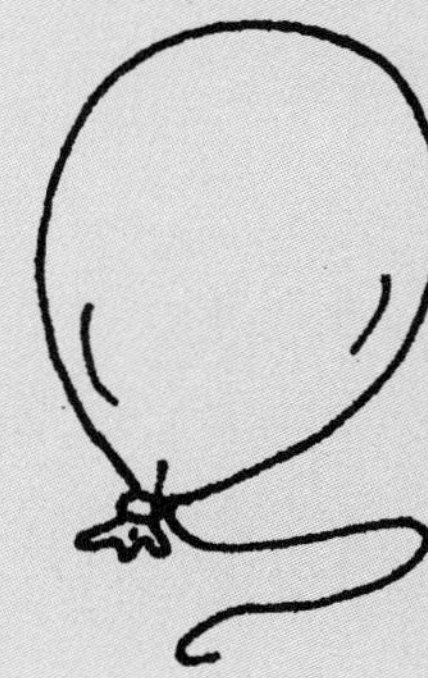

Love, Liz

⑥ **Read the questions and complete the answers.**

1. Why does Liz write invitation cards?
   Because it's her ______________________________.
2. Why do they need pyjamas and brushes?
   Because it's a ______________________________.
3. Why don't they go to the park?
   Because they go ______________________________.
4. Why does Liz's mother go shopping?
   Because they need sausages, ______________, ______________________.
5. Why do they need their swimsuits?
   Because she ______________________________.

⑦ **When is your party and what do you want to do? Write five sentences about your next birthday party.**

My birthday party ______________________________

____

____

1 food - Übersichtsseite

apple (Apfel)

pear (Birne)

pineapple (Ananas)

salad (Salat)

onion (Zwiebel)

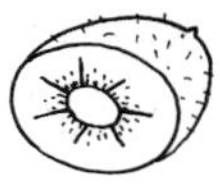
kiwi (Kiwi)

chicken / meat (Hühnchen / Fleisch)

eggs (Eier), scrambled eggs (Rührei), fried eggs (Spiegeleier)

cake (Kuchen)

cornflakes (Cornflakes)

tea (Tee)

orange juice (Orangensaft)

fish (Fisch)

banana (Banane)

strawberry (Erdbeere)

cherry (Kirsche)

carrot (Karotte)

cucumber (Gurke)

grapes (Trauben)

fruit (Obst)

jam (Marmelade)

toast (Toast)

cereals (Müsli)

coffee (Kaffee)

water (Wasser)

vegetables (Gemüse)

pea (Erbse)

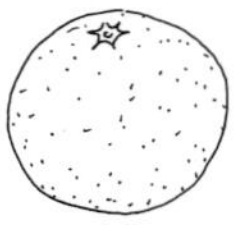
orange (Orange)

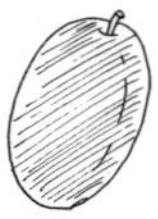
plum (Pflaume)

potato (Kartoffel)

tomato (Tomate)

peach (Pfirsich)

cheese (Käse)

sausage (Wurst)

butter (Butter)

bread (Brot)

milk (Milch)

rolls (Brötchen)

honey (Honig)

10

food 1

1 What do the animals eat? Write down the correct words.
Was essen die Tiere? Schreibe die Wörter richtig auf.

1. Cats eat *(shif)* <u>*fish*</u>.
2. Dogs eat *(atem)* ________________ and *(agessaus)* ________________.
3. Hamsters eat *(rrotsca)* ________________.
4. Parrots eat *(alads)* ________________.
5. Horses eat *(lesapp)* ________________.
6. Mice eat *(eseche)* ________________.

2 What you need for your food
Use the pictures and the words in the box to complete the sentences.
Vervollständige die Sätze mithilfe der Bilder und der Wörter in der Box.

1. I eat cornflakes out of a **bowl**. 
2. I drink orange juice out of a ________________. 
3. I eat chips from a ________________. 
4. We buy water in a ________________. 
5. When I watch TV I eat a ________________ of crisps. 
6. My mum puts all fruits in a ________________.  .
7. We buy eggs in a ________________. 
8. My brother eats a ________________ of chocolate every day. 
9. My dad drinks coffee out of a ________________. 

basket, Korb – box, Schachtel – bar, Tafel – cup, Tasse – bag, Tüte –
bottle, Flasche – plate, Teller – glass, Glas – ~~bowl, Schüssel~~

10 food 2

3 Fruits and vegetables

a) What fruits do you know? Look at the pictures and write down the words. Use the ideas from the box. There are 10 words but you only need 8.

Welche Früchte kennst du? Schau dir die Bilder an und schreibe die Wörter. Du kannst die Ideen in der Box verwenden. Dort stehen 10 Wörter, aber du brauchst nur 8.

 ______________________

 ______________________

 ______________________

 ______________________

 ______________________

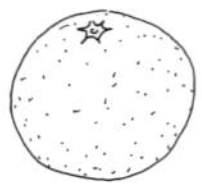 ______________________

 ______________________

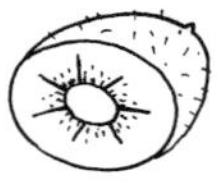 ______________________

peach – pineapple – apple – banana – potato – grapes – orange – strawberry – kiwi – pear

b) What vegetables do you know? Look at the pictures and write down the words. You can use the ideas in the box. There are 7 words but you only need 6.

Welche Gemüsesorten kennst du? Schau dir die Bilder an und schreibe die Wörter. Du kannst die Ideen in der Box verwenden. Dort stehen 7 Wörter, du brauchst aber nur 6.

 ______________________

 ______________________

 ______________________

 ______________________

 ______________________

 ______________________

onion – potato – salad – tomato – carrot – cucumber – peach

10 food 3

4 Look at Tony's breakfast. What does he like? And what doesn't he like? Tick the right answer.
Schau dir Tonys Frühstückstisch an. Was mag er, was mag er nicht? Kreuze die richtige Antwort an.

1. Tony likes cake. ☐
2. Tony likes hot chocolate. ☐
3. Tony doesn't like cornflakes. ☐
4. Tony doesn't like sausages. ☐
5. Tony likes bananas. ☐
6. Tony likes rolls. ☐
7. Tony likes boiled eggs. ☐
8. Tony doesn't like orange juice. ☐
9. Tony likes toast. ☐
10. Tony likes potatoes. ☐
11. Tony likes cheese. ☐
12. Tony doesn't like sandwiches. ☐
13. Tony doesn't like fruit salad. ☐
14. Tony likes tea. ☐
15. Tony likes chicken. ☐
16. Tony likes tomatoes. ☐

5 What do you like? Write 8 sentences about what you eat.
Welches Essen magst du? Ergänze die 8 Sätze.

1. I like ______________________________
2. I don't like ______________________________
3. I often have ______________________________ for breakfast.
4. At the weekend I have ______________________________ for breakfast.
5. I don't eat ______________________________
6. I never eat ______________________________
7. I don't like ______________________________
8. I like ______________________________

10 food 4

6 Write questions for your friend and ask him or her. You can use the ideas in the box or your own words.

Schreibe Fragen für deinen Freund / deine Freundin und stelle sie. Du kannst die Ideen in der Box verwenden oder eigene Wörter wählen.

You ask:	**Your friend answers:**
1. Do you like tomatoes?	Yes, I do / No, I don't.
2. Do you like ______?	______.
3. ______?	______.
4. ______?	______.
5. ______?	______.
6. ______?	______.
7. ______?	______.
8. ______?	______.
9. ______?	______.
10. ______?	______.

cheese, cucumber, tea, water, orange juice, coffee, rolls, fried eggs, toast, apples, bananas, oranges, cornflakes, cake, biscuit, crisps, chips, ~~tomatoes~~, potatoes

7 What can you eat or drink? Make a list. You can use the ideas in the box or your own words.

Was kannst du essen oder trinken? Erstelle eine Liste. Du kannst die Ideen in der Box verwenden oder eigene Wörter wählen.

I can eat	I can drink
cheese	water

apple, banana, pea, pear, strawberry, orange, tea, coffee, milk, cherry, salad, carrot, potato, cucumber, tomato, kiwi, peach, fried eggs, jam, sausages, cake, toast, butter, cornflakes, orange juice, ~~water~~, chicken / meat, fruit, ~~cheese~~, fish

10 food 5

8 Match the words and the pictures.

(water)

(cornflakes)

(chocolate)

(crisps)

(apples)

(orange juice)

(eggs)

bottle (2x) – bowl – bar – basket – box – bag

a bottle of water

9 Find the fruits and vegetables.
Finde das Obst und Gemüse.

T	G	Q	R	R	B	X	G	S	O	S	D	C	F	C	G	H
Q	C	J	B	O	N	I	O	N	L	T	K	Q	P	F	S	Y
W	D	Y	P	R	X	C	U	O	E	R	H	V	E	S	A	R
I	H	U	W	J	M	W	Y	O	O	A	O	N	A	E	L	X
T	R	G	F	P	F	T	W	C	K	W	I	B	F	M	A	U
P	P	A	O	G	D	O	L	A	P	B	D	C	X	X	D	Y
L	I	N	R	O	L	M	P	R	B	E	Q	H	H	R	B	T
P	N	U	A	Y	Z	A	T	R	C	R	R	E	X	Q	F	Y
J	E	H	N	N	O	T	H	O	B	R	D	R	P	P	B	M
W	A	R	G	K	G	O	T	T	B	Y	V	R	I	E	G	W
P	P	R	E	D	J	E	F	U	N	V	W	Y	U	A	Z	B
H	P	H	S	P	B	G	D	P	C	O	O	D	Q	R	L	A
O	L	K	F	F	R	G	U	O	D	J	N	D	F	K	M	N
F	E	K	O	R	C	U	C	U	M	B	E	R	B	B	G	A
R	M	V	X	W	B	G	F	X	S	J	J	U	P	P	U	N
R	P	O	T	A	T	O	E	Q	E	A	P	P	L	E	G	A
R	Y	U	M	H	X	K	R	B	P	X	Q	P	N	T	G	A

pea, apple,
banana, cucumber,
salad, tomato,
potato, pear,
strawberry, cherry,
orange, pineapple,
carrot, onion

food 6

What Sarah loves to eat and drink.

Read the text and tick the right answer.

Lies den Text und kreuze die richtige Antwort an.

Sarah loves fruit and vegetables. Her favourite drink is not water. She loves lemonade. When she watches TV, she always eats an apple. That's very healthy. In the restaurant she orders pizza and salad. She loves tomatoes. Her mother always says that she needs a garden full of tomatoes. Of course Sarah loves chocolate, too. Her grandmother makes the best chocolate cake.

What does Sarah love?	fruit ☐	shoes ☐
What is her favourite drink?	milk ☐	lemonade ☐
What does she eat in the restaurant?	spaghetti ☐	pizza ☐
Why does she eat salad?	because of the tomatoes ☐	because of the chocolate ☐
What does Sarah love?	chocolate ☐	jam ☐
Who makes the best chocolate cake?	Liz ☐	Liz's grandmother ☐

10 food 1

① **What do the animals eat? Look at the pictures and make sentences.**

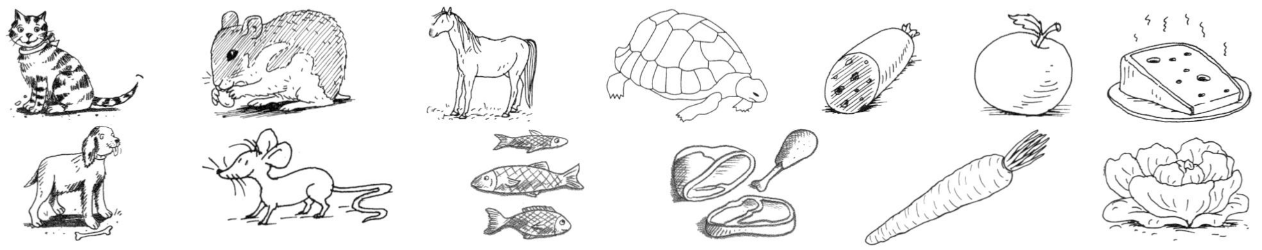

1. Cats eat fish.
2. Dogs eat ______________________________
3. ______________________________
4. ______________________________
5. ______________________________
6. ______________________________

② **What you need for your food**

Fill the gaps. Use the pictures and complete the sentences.

1.  2.  3.  4.  5. 

6.  7.  8.  9. 

1. I eat cornflakes out of a **bowl.**
2. I drink orange juice out of a ________________.
3. I eat chips from a ________________.
4. We buy water in a ________________.
5. When I watch TV I eat a ________________ of crisps.
6. My mum puts all fruits in a ________________.
7. We buy eggs in a ________________.
8. My brother eats a ________________ of chocolate every day.
9. My dad drinks coffee out of a ________________.

10 food 2

③ **Fruits and vegetables**

a) What fruits do you know? Look at the pictures and write down the words.

 ______________________  ______________________

 ______________________ 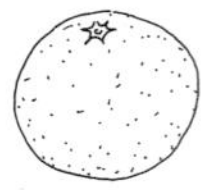 ______________________

 ______________________  ______________________

 ______________________ 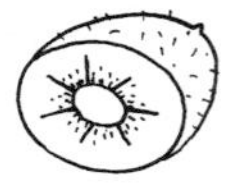 ______________________

b) What vegetables do you know? Look at the pictures and write down the words.

 ______________________  ______________________

 ______________________  ______________________

 ______________________  ______________________

④ **Look at Tony's breakfast. What does he like? And what doesn't he like? Write sentences on an extra sheet of paper.**

what Tony likes	what Tony doesn't like

1. Tony likes rolls.	1. Tony doesn't like cucumber.
2. Tony likes ...	2. Tony doesn't like ...

food 3

⑤ **What do you like? Write eight sentences about what you eat. You can start your sentences like this:**

I like ... / I don't like ... / I often have ... / At the weekend I eat ...

1. ______________________
2. ______________________
3. ______________________
4. ______________________
5. ______________________
6. ______________________
7. ______________________
8. ______________________

⑥ **What does your friend like? Write questions for your friend and ask him or her.**

You ask:	Your friend answers:
1. Do you like tomatoes?	Yes, I do / No, I don't.
2. Do you like ______________?	______________
3. ______________?	______________
4. ______________?	______________
5. ______________?	______________
6. ______________?	______________
7. ______________?	______________
8. ______________?	______________

⑦ **What can you eat? What can you drink? Make a list.**

I can eat	I can drink
butter	water

10 food 4

⑧ **Match the words.**

bowl, basket, bar, bottle (2x), bag, box, orange juice,
appples, cornflakes, eggs, water, crisps, chocolate

a bottle of water

____

____

____

⑨ **Find the fruits and vegetables.**

E	M	U	H	M	T	N	Z	M	Q	K	F	D	K	D	H	S	F	V
Q	F	Z	C	S	K	O	R	A	N	G	E	F	V	R	U	F	C	F
C	T	B	H	H	M	E	Q	J	O	P	E	D	M	T	R	H	S	W
O	N	I	O	N	M	I	N	W	W	G	U	J	M	D	P	C	R	V
B	F	C	B	J	X	U	R	X	S	S	A	L	A	D	F	M	Q	Z
A	B	U	J	O	M	V	O	S	N	F	S	H	M	P	E	A	Q	I
N	V	C	Y	J	C	D	V	T	O	M	A	T	O	E	N	O	N	J
A	L	U	X	R	T	E	L	F	P	I	N	E	A	P	P	L	E	N
N	M	M	W	E	P	E	B	B	R	F	H	J	D	Q	P	T	B	F
A	W	B	W	T	F	V	C	K	F	N	S	E	I	V	O	O	X	F
Y	G	E	X	N	U	B	A	Q	S	J	T	R	U	J	T	Y	F	E
G	U	R	S	S	V	R	R	C	Q	P	R	K	R	S	A	Z	W	J
E	E	W	W	T	G	V	R	W	N	D	A	X	B	M	T	L	N	M
C	C	S	O	Q	G	W	O	Y	M	F	W	G	O	L	O	H	K	Q
X	H	H	I	P	S	K	T	V	O	G	B	D	U	M	E	S	V	Z
J	C	H	E	R	R	Y	R	P	W	U	E	I	J	K	M	B	X	W
X	O	O	Y	S	Z	A	P	P	L	E	R	J	X	J	K	X	J	T
J	C	I	Y	U	H	P	C	F	Z	Q	R	O	O	R	P	E	A	R
X	M	Q	E	D	Q	E	Q	D	D	D	Y	Q	F	B	P	Y	M	O

pea, apple, banana,
cucumber, salad, tomato,
potato, pear, strawberry,
cherry, orange, pineapple,
carrot, onion

⑩ **What Sarah loves to eat and drink**
Read the text and answer the questions.

Sarah loves fruit and vegetables. Her favourite drink is not water. She loves lemonade. When she watches TV, she always eats an apple. That's very healthy. In the restaurant she orders pizza and salad. She loves tomatoes. Her mother always says that she needs a garden full of tomatoes. Of course Sarah loves chocolate, too. Her grandmother makes the best chocolate cake.

What is her favourite drink? ______________________

What does she eat in the restaurant? ______________________

Why does she eat salad? ______________________

What does Sarah love? ______________________

Who makes the best chocolate cake? ______________________

11 shopping and clothes - Übersichtsseite

blazer (Blazer), suit (Anzug), school uniform (Schuluniform)

shirt (Hemd)

T-shirt (T-Shirt)

tie (Krawatte)

skirt (Rock)

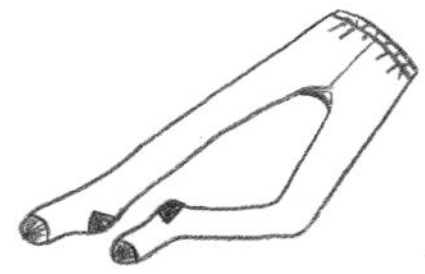
tights (Strumpfhose)

trainers (Sportschuhe)

shoes (Schuhe)

sandals (Sandalen)

pullover (Pullover)

blouse (Bluse)

socks (Socken)

swimsuit (Badeanzug)

shorts (kurze Hose)

sunglasses (Sonnenbrille)

hat (Hut)

dress (Kleid)

trousers / jeans (Hose / Jeans)

boots (Stiefel)

jacket (Jacke)

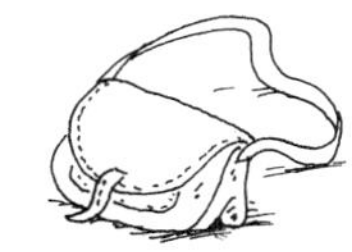
bag (Tasche)

size (Größe)

small (kleines T-Shirt)

medium (mittleres T-Shirt)

large (großes T-Shirt)

11 shopping and clothes 1

1 ▸ Look at the pictures. What can you see? Name the clothes.
Schau dir die Bilder an. Was siehst du? Benenne die Kleidungsstücke.

2 ▸ How much are the jeans? Look at the shop. Make questions on an extra sheet of paper and answer them. Use the words from the box.
Schau dir den Laden an. Bilde Fragen und beantworte sie. Verwende die Wörter in der Box.

1. How much are the jeans? The jeans are 15 euros.
2. How much is the pullover? The pullover is ...

T-shirt, ~~pullover~~, shoes, caps, ~~jeans~~, skirts, dresses, blouses

11 shopping and clothes 2

3 What clothes do you know? Find the words and write them in the gaps.
Finde die Wörter und schreibe sie in die Lücken.

 d _ _ _ s

 s _ _ _ s

 t _ _ _ _ _ _ s

 s _ _ _ t

 b _ _ _ s

 s _ _ t

 s _ _ _ s

 p _ _ _ _ _ _ r

 s _ _ _ _ s

 t _ e

4 Name the shop and write the word over the picture. Write down what you can buy there. The words in the box can help you.
Schreibe den Namen des Ladens über das Bild. Schreibe auf, was du dort kaufen kannst. Verwende die Begriffe aus der Box.

bag shop, sports shop, shoe shop
school bags, hand bags, boots, basketballs, trainers, shorts, footballs, suitcases, high heels, T-shirts

44 shopping and clothes 3

5 Read the text and tick the right answer.
Lies den Text und kreuze die richtige Antwort an.

Shopping for the party

Tomorrow is the birthday party of Sarah's best friend. She wants to look beautiful.

But she has nothing special in her wardrobe.

She goes shopping. She needs new shoes, new jeans and a nice T-shirt.

In the shop Sarah finds many nice clothes and a dress.

She thinks about the dress, but then she finds a nice T-shirt and nice shoes.

She tries the T-shirt on and she likes it, because it is her favourite colour.

She is happy, because all is her size.

She buys the shoes and the T-shirt and goes home.

The party can start now …

1. Whose birthday is tomorrow?	Sarah's birthday ☐	Sarah's best friend ☐
2. What does Sarah do?	goes shopping ☐	goes to school ☐
3. What does she find in the shop?	nice clothes ☐	a cat ☐
4. What does she buy?	shoes and a T-shirt ☐	a dress and a T-shirt ☐
5. Why does she like the T-shirt?	It is her favourite colour. ☐	It's cheap. ☐

11 shopping and clothes 4

6 In English please. Match the German and the English sentences.
Füge die englischen und die deutschen Sätze zusammen.

① Sam: Entschuldigung. Wo kann ich das T-Shirt anprobieren?

◯ Verkäufer: Da drüben. Neben den Taschen.

◯ Verkäufer: Kein Problem. Wir haben auch andere Farben da. Welche ist deine Lieblingsfarbe?

◯ Over there. Next to the bags.

◯ Thank you. The size is right, but I don't like the colour.

◯ No problem, we've got other colours, too. What is your favourite colour?

◯ My favourite colour is blue. Thank you.

◯ Sam: Blau ist meine Lieblingsfarbe. Danke.

◯ Sam: Dankeschön. Die Größe stimmt, aber ich mag die Farbe nicht.

① Excuse me. Where can I try on this T-shirt?

7 How much is it? Ask the questions and write down the answers.
Wie teuer sind die Sachen? Notiere die Fragen und Antworten.

12 €

25 €

30 €

50 €

15 €

20 €

A: *How much is the swimsuit?*

B: *It's 25 €.*

A: How much is the ______________?

B: It's ______________

A: How much is the ______________?

B: It's ______________

A: *How much are the trainers?*

B: *They are 50 €.*

A: How much is the ______________?

B: It's ______________

A: How much are the ______________?

B: They are ______________

11 shopping and clothes 1

(1) **What do they wear? Look at the pictures. What can you see? Name the clothes.**

____
____
____
____

____
____
____
____

(2) **How much are the jeans? Look at the shop. Make questions on an extra sheet of paper and answer them.**

1. How much are the jeans? The jeans are 15 euros.

(3) **What clothes do you know? Find the words and write them in the blankets.**

 d _ _ _ s

 s _ _ _ s

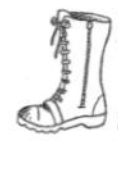 t _ _ _ _ _ _ s

 s _ _ _ t

 b _ _ _ s

 s _ _ t

 s _ _ _ s

 p _ _ _ _ _ _ r

 s _ _ _ _ s

 t _ e

11

shopping and clothes 2

④ **What's the name of the shop? Write down two things you can buy there.**

⑤ **Shopping for the party**

Tomorrow is the birthday party of Sarah's best friend. She wants to look beautiful. But she has nothing special in her wardrobe. She goes shopping. She needs new shoes, new jeans and a nice T-shirt. In the shop Sarah finds many nice clothes and a dress. She thinks about the dress, but then she finds a nice T-shirt and nice shoes. She tries the T-shirt on and she likes it, because it is her favourite colour. She is happy, because all is her size. She buys the shoes and the T-shirt and goes home. The party can start now …

1. Whose birthday is tomorrow? ____________________
2. What does Sarah do? ____________________
3. What does she find in the shop? ____________________
4. What does she buy? ____________________
5. Why does she like the T-shirt? ____________________

shopping and clothes 3

(6) **In English please. Translate the sentences.**

Sam: Entschuldigung. Wo kann ich das T-Shirt anprobieren?

______

______

Verkäufer: Da drüben. Neben den Taschen.

______

______

Sam: Dankeschön. Die Größe stimmt, aber ich mag die Farbe nicht.

______

______

Verkäufer: Kein Problem. Wir haben auch andere Farben. Welche ist deine Lieblingsfarbe?

______

______

______

Sam: Blau ist meine Lieblingsfarbe. Danke.

______

______

(7) **How much is it? Ask the questions and write down the answers.**

swimsuit: 25 €

How much is the swimsuit?

- It's 25 €.

jeans: 15 €

______

______

trainers: 50 €

How much are ______

______

jacket: 30 €

______

______

bag: 20 €

______

______

T-shirt: 12 €

______

______

11

shopping and clothes 4

⑧ **Fill in the missing words. Translate first!**

Sportgeschäft – ____________

Größe – ____________

medium – ____________

T-Shirts – ____________

Geschenk – ____________

Lieblings – ____________

kurze Hose – ____________

Mrs Tailor goes to a ____________.
She wants to buy a ____________ for
Sam's birthday. It is his ____________
shop. He always buys ____________
and ____________ there.
The ____________ of the T-shirt is
____________ and it's 25 €.

⑨ **Shopping in your town.**

Write four sentences about shopping. What are your favourite shops? What do you buy there?

Start like this.

My favourite shops are …

I buy ... there

____

____

____

____

____

____

____

Abbildungsverzeichnis

Mehrfach verwendete Illustrationen sind nur bei Erstabbildung genannt.

Cover und Kapitelpiktogramme: Stefan Lucas; **S. 8** Frau mit V-Ausschnitt: Julia Flasche, alle weiteren Personen und Symbole: Barbara Gerth; **S. 10** Familie / Mutter und Tochter: Barbara Gerth; **S. 15** Familienstammbaum: Barbara Gerth; **S. 18** Sofa / Sessel / Tisch / Vorhänge / Regal / Kleiderschrank / Bett / Dusche / Waschbecken / Spiegel / Toilette / Stuhl / Schrank / Herd / Kühlschrank: Oliver Wetterauer, Teppich / Schreibtisch / Lampe: Barbara Gerth, Waschmaschine © Sashkin – Fotolia.com, Geschirrspülmaschine © photosvac – Fotolia.com; **S. 19** Handy / CD: Mele Brink, T-Shirt: Katharina Reichert-Scarborough, Rucksack: Barbara Gerth, Buch: Alexandra Hanneforth, Filzstift: Julia Flasche, Querschnitt Haus: Barbara Gerth; **S. 21** Haus: Barbara Gerth; **S. 22** Beide Kinderzimmer: Barbara Gerth; **S. 23** Tür: Mele Brink, TV: Oliver Wetterauer; **S. 29** Sonne: Anke Fröhlich, Mädchen „Thank you.“: Stefan Lucas, Fenster: Barbara Gerth, „Open your book…“ / „Don't talk! / „Listen!“: Mele Brink, „Be quiet, please.“: Julia Flasche, Etui / Füller: Julia Flasche, Radiergummi / Schultasche / Lineal / Anspitzer / Bleistift: Barbara Gerth, Heft: Theresia Koppers; **S. 34** Wasserflasche: Jennifer Spry, Smartphone © vege – Fotolia.com, Apfel: Barbara Gerth, Ball: Gunkel Claessen, Butterbrot: Thomas Binder; **S. 35** Sandwich: Barbara Gerth; **S. 36** Zauberer: Stefan Lucas; **S. 38** Schule: Bert Breitenbach, Turnhalle: Barbara Gerth, Hausmeisterraum: Oliver Wetterauer; **S. 45** Fußball / Baskteball / Pferd / Inliner / Computer / tanzen / Briefmarke / Fahrrad / malen: Barbara Gerth, Klavier / singen / lesen / Badeanzug: Katharina Reichert-Scarborough, Schlittschuhe: Mele Brink, Tennis: Julia Flasche, Judo: Kerrin Paulsen, Ski: Sven Lehmkuhl, Musik hören: Oliver Wetterauer; **S. 46** Karten: Stefan Lucas, schwimmen: Barbara Gerth; **S. 48** Janet bei verschiedenen Tätigkeiten: Barbara Gerth; **S. 51** Gitarre: Gunkel Claessen; **S. 55** Fisch / Schlange / Bär / Giraffe / Affe / Zebra / Elefant / Tiger: Katharina Reichert-Scarborough, Korb / Käfig / Hamster / Vogel / Kaninchen / Papagei / Maus / Kuh / Schwein / Gans / Schaf / Krokodil, Aquarium: Claudia Bauer, Schildkröte: Gunkel Claessen, Wellensittich: Oliver Wetterauer, Meerschweinchen © mdxphoto – Fotolia.com; **S. 59** Auf dem Hof: Katharina Reichert-Scarborough; **S. 64** Milch: Anke Fröhlich, Wolle: Eckart Breitschuh, Huhn / Eier / Wurst / Feder: Barbara Gerth; **S. 65** Schneemann / Clown / Osterei / Maiglöckchen / Regen / Tannenbaum: Barbara Gerth, Vogel: Alexandra Hanneforth, Sonnenblume: Andrea Frick-Snuggs, Strand, Igel: Marion El-Khalafawi, Halloween: Nataly Meenen; **S. 75** Wecker: Barbara Gerth; **S. 77** Frühstück: Julia Flasche, Fußabdrücke: Ingrid Hecht, TV: Oliver Wetterauer; **S. 85** Farbpalette: Mele Brink, Bär: Julia Flasche; **S. 86** Junge auf Fahrrad, Kinderzimmer: Barbara Gerth; **S. 89** Torte / Kerze: Mele Brink, Happy Birthday: Bert Breitenbach, Einladung: Nataly Meenen, Geschenk / Kuchen / Kekse: Barbara Gerth, Ballons / Geburtstagsliste / Getränk: Julia Flasche, Gäste: Daniela Bühnen, Musik: Oliver Wetterauer; **S. 90** Geburtstagstisch: Barbara Gerth; **S. 91** Bilder auf Einladungen: Barbara Gerth; **S. 96** Apfel / Banane / Erbsen / Birne / Erdbeere / Orange / Ananas / Kirschen / Pflaume / Salat / Kartoffeln / Gurke / Tomate / Trauben / Pfirsich / Obst / Käse / Marmelade / Toast / Brot / Brötchen / Butter: Barbara Gerth, Karotte / Zwiebel: Jennifer Spry, Kiwi / Gemüse: Julia Flasche, Fleisch: Katharina Reichert-Scarborough, Cornflakes / Müsli: Sabine Mohrmann, Tee / Kaffee: Mele Brink, Orangensaft: © seralex – Fotolia.com; **S. 97** Schälchen / Korb / Schokolade: Barbara Gerth, Glas: Julia Flasche, Teller: Alexandra Hanneforth, Chips: Theresia Koppers; **S. 99** Junge am Tisch: Barbara Gerth; **S. 107** Blazer: Daniela Bühnen, Hemd: Oliver Wetterauer, Rock / Strumpfhose / Sportschuhe / Schuhe / Sandalen / Pullover / Bluse / Socke / kurze Hose / Kleid / Jeans / Stiefel / Jacke: Katharina Reichert-Scarborough, Krawatte: Julia Flasche, Sonnenbrille: Nataly Meenen, Tasche: Barbara Gerth, Hut: Jennifer Spry; **S. 108** Mädchen / Junge / Kleidung: Barbara Gerth; **S. 109** Schaufenster: Barbara Gerth; **S. 110** Sarah beim Shoppen: Barbara Gerth; **S. 115** Einkaufsstraße: Barbara Gerth